A CHALLENGE TO THE REMNANT!

A CHALLENGE TO THE REMNANT!

*DESIGNING OUR MISSION STRATEGY
TO IMPACT THE REAL WORLD*

Ruthven J. Roy

REHOBOTH
PUBLISHING

Copyright © 2002, 2017 by Ruthven J. Roy

A Challenge To The Remnant: Designing Our Mission Strategy to Impact the Real World.

ISBN: Paperback 978-0-9888132-6-7
0-9888132-6-2

Cover design: Emmerson Cyrille

All rights reserved. No part of this book may be reproduced or transmitted in any form or by any means without permission in writing from the copyright owner.

Unless otherwise stated, Scripture texts are from the Holy Bible, *The Authorized King James Version*, copyright © 1975 by Thomas Nelson Inc. Publishers, and used by permission. All rights are reserved.

Other versions used are

NASB - *New American Standard Bible*, © 1960, 1962, 1963, 1968, 1971, 1972, 1973, 1975, 1977, by the Lockman Foundation. Used by permission of AMG Publishers.

NRSV - *New Revised Standard Version*, © 1989 by the Division of Christian Education of the National Council of the Churches of Christ in the United States of America. Used by permission.

Printed in the United States of America

Rehoboth Publishing
P.O. Box 33
Berrien Springs, MI 49103

To contact the author, email: ruthvenroy@gmail.com or visit, www.roybooks.com

Contents

Foreword v
A word to the reader vii
Acknowledgments ix
Introduction xi

Chapters

1. Saving the lost: God's mission not ours 15

2. Remnant theology and the shaping of our mission strategy 27

3. God's mission and the remnant mind-set 37

4. A mind-set for God's mission 65

5. Shifting our mission paradigm 113

6. Mission and ministry relevance 151

7. Toward a more strategic approach 189

8. Mission beyond adventism 219

Conclusion 263

Appendix 271

Foreword
by
Dr. Walter Douglas

*I*n this book, Dr. Ruthven Roy gives us a new and refreshing look at the central reason for the church's existence in the world. In a masterful and compelling way, he challenges us to examine every church structure and every activity in the light of one searching question—Does it contribute to God's mission in the world? The church, he insists, exists for mission, and therefore, everything about the church—its worship, its fellowship, its polity—are all ways in which the church fulfills this central task.

If the church envisions itself with a destiny and a future apart from mission, it will become disoriented and utterly dysfunctional. As Leslie Newbigin puts it: "The church is the pilgrim people of God, and hastening to the end of time to meet its Lord who will gather all into one. . . by the End to which it moves." So until the end of time, mission is our calling.

Dr. Roy quite correctly focuses our attention on Christology as the foundation and structure of Adventist mission. The mission of God begins with God sending His Son into the world to seek and save the lost. This biblical and theological doctrine was, and remains, the vision and engine that drive Seventh-day Adventist mission. Roy challenges the church to return and remain faithful to this core teaching, but he does so in creative, imaginative ways that are very

FOREWORD

relevant to our times.

In chapters 6 and 7, he articulates this stimulating approach to mission by what he describes and analyzes as "market sensitive mission and ministry." Here he states, "Mission always puts people before policies, procedures and politics . . . Mission is a people priority." Consequently, Roy develops and recommends strategies for reaching people that are very crucial for the success of our mission in the 21st century.

These two chapters by themselves make this book an invaluable resource for anyone who has a serious interest in dealing with the complex challenges of doing mission in an increasingly multicultural and diverse world.

So if you are wondering whether there is room for yet another book on Adventist mission in the 21st century, this book answers that question without any ambiguity as it explores the basic affirmation of the Christian faith, and its implication for the church's call to mission and ministry.

Walter B.T. Douglas (retired 2005) was the Chair of the Church History Department and Professor of History of Religions at the Seventh-day Adventist Theological Seminary, located on the campus of Andrews University, Berrien Springs, Michigan, USA.

A Word To The Reader
by
My Mentor
(Dr. K. S. Wiggins)

At last someone has found the courage to tell the SDA Church that in order for a message to have impact, it must be presented without ambivalence, and must be seen, by the audience, as relevant and important and urgent!!

Readers are urged to read this book with an open mind, although doing so will be difficult. It will be difficult because an appreciation of the information will be based on personality factors, power struggles, social psychological processes, defense mechanisms, cultural influences, theological biases, and the spirit of the age.

It is difficult for people with the Adventist mind-set to realize fully that successful evangelism does not depend on spiritual dynamics only, but psycho-social and cultural dynamics play an important role.

The author of this book is challenging the Church to greater success by re-evaluating its true mission, to cease seeing Jewish and first century gentile problems as the exact image of our own problems, and to perform ministry in ways that are theologically defensible, and strategically shrewd.

So, if this book aids in advancing the kingdom of God and the true mission of Christians, then it will have done the Church a great service.

Kembleton S. Wiggins is a Social Psychologist, Evangelist, and Therapist in Cleburne, Texas, USA Michigan, USA

Acknowledgments

The writing of this volume would not have been possible without the invaluable contributions of a few very important people. First and foremost, I wish to thank my dear wife Lyris Roy for her sacrifice, support and reflective insight that have positively influenced the outcome of this book. I also wish to thank our lovely daughters, Charisa, Lyrisa, and Mirisa for allowing me the privilege to dedicate so much time to this project.

Likewise, I wish to acknowledge Emmerson "Emmo" Cyrille for the immaculate cover and interior design of this book. I could always count on him for exceptional outcomes. My gratitude to Marilyn Bell-Joseph for her excellent editorial work in this revised edition, and for her honesty and timely suggestions in producing the final draft of this manuscript.

I am sincerely appreciative of the contributions of Dr. Walter B.T. Douglas who wrote the foreword to the book, and for the editorial comments and encouragement of Doctors Russell Staples, George Knight and Bruce Bauer. Special thanks go to my mentor, Dr. Kembleton S. Wiggins for writing a word to the readers of this volume, and for his intellectual stimulation that helped me to develop into a free thinker. I am also indebted to my dear friend Dr. Ernan Norman for his reflective insight and helpful input in producing this book.

Above all I acknowledge and give thanks to God, by

ACKNOWLEDGMENTS

whose wisdom and kindness I have been able to accomplish this work for the cause of Christ.

Introduction

*B*ecause of the many positive responses from readers of this book, I have chosen to review and expand on the ideas, principles and truths I discussed and explored in the first printing. While the basic message of the book has not changed, I have made some worthwhile adjustments that have strengthened the case for this book to be a very important tool for present-day Adventist evangelism.

In this volume I have made an honest attempt to examine how we think about and perform mission as a community of faith. Admittedly, such honesty can be very painful and costly (as some readers have confessed), but there is no other path to honest self-discovery, positive change and real, meaningful progress. I have looked at our self-understanding in the context of our remnant theology, and have shown how this self-understanding has created a typical Adventist mind-set that has impacted our philosophy and practice of mission. Some readers may find the examination of this mind-set very difficult, at first, since it exposes some sensitive nerves within the Adventist psyche, but further reading will justify the need for such exposure as we seek to effectively meet the mission challenges facing our church.

Furthermore, I have looked at some of our traditional approaches to evangelism and have suggested some alternative ways of thinking and working in our efforts to reach all kinds of spiritually lost people. In order to

INTRODUCTION

accomplish this purpose, I have introduced three powerful concepts that can bring significant transformation and profound success to our mission and ministry endeavors. First among these is the idea of doing mission and ministry from a creative, strategic perspective to increase individual and organizational efficiency and effectiveness. As such, the *strategic mission/ministry planning process* (SMPP) is a very useful tool to guide the local church or larger organization in achieving its mission and ministry objectives and goals.

Second, is the concept of performing mission from *outside in*, instead of the traditional approach of pursuing mission from *inside out*. Mission from inside out is shaped by a preoccupation with *organizational needs, doctrinal beliefs, plans and goals, with little or no consideration for the needs of the target audience*. On the other hand, mission from outside in begins with a striving to understand the needs and present circumstances of the target audience, and then designing an approach (in terms of message and methodology) that will connect effectively with that audience. This will make our mission and ministry approaches more relevant to the needs of the target communities and increase our ability to influence them for the Kingdom of God.

The third concept, Network Discipling, is a revolutionary distribution idea for exponentially multiplying fruit-bearing disciples throughout the believing community. However, a full exploration of this last concept will require more space than this volume will allow. I have given this

INTRODUCTION

subject a more thorough treatment in another one of my publications, *"The Explosive Power of Network Discipling"*[1].

Additionally, I have portrayed Jesus Christ as the Dynamic Center of God's mission enterprise, and have challenged every reader never to attempt to change or replace this Center by any other. We must resist at all cost, the alluring temptation to elevate and emphasize the name of the Church, it message, or claim to "remnancy" above the claims and the person of Christ in all our ministry and evangelistic efforts.

In conclusion, it is my sincere pray for all my readers, that the contents of this book would challenge and change your personal understanding, thinking and actions as those relate to our Master's call upon us as His disciples and ambassadors in this world. After all, mission is God's enterprise, and following Jesus' lead is the only way to accomplish the task to the honor and glory of His name.

Note

1. Ruthven J. Roy, *The Explosive Power of Network Discipling* (Berrien Spring, MI: Rehoboth Publishing, 2010).

1

SAVING THE LOST: GOD'S MISSION, NOT OURS

The *Missio Dei* (the Mission of God) embraces all the divine-human activities involved in carrying out God's redemptive purpose in the world, and has as its ultimate objective the complete reconciliation and restoration of the earth and the human race. Mission was born in the heart of a loving God who, in His divine wisdom and foreknowledge, devised a plan from the foundation of the world (Rev 13:8), to take care of the catastrophic emergence of sin. Our God is a missionary God![1] Yet, while the well-spring of the *Missio Dei* is divine love, the reason for that mission was man's utter lostness and dire need of a Savior. Ellen White[2] states, the Son of God, heaven's glorious Commander, was touched with pity for the fallen race. His heart was moved with infinite compassion as the woes of the lost world rose up before Him."[3] In the mysterious counsel of peace (Zech 6:13), Christ offered up Himself as man's substitute and sacrifice before the foundation of the earth was laid (Rev 13:8).

The *Missio Dei*, then, grew out of mankind's disobedience, downfall, and impending doom, and God's loving response in expending heaven's best resources to save His creation. Darrell L. Guder states, "the compassion of God is the motivating power of God's mission. Both God's act of creation and God's determination to heal His rebellious creation are the compelling reasons for the salvation history which unfolds from Abraham onward."[4] The fall of the human race created an urgent *need* in the universe, and Christ embarked upon a mission of death in order to *satisfy* this need. It took one equal with God to pay the enormous price for man's redemption. From the moment man sinned, the missionary God left the glories of heaven and came down to the benighted planet, seeking after him: "*Adam where are you?*" (Gen 3:9). It was in the context of this very first mission enterprise that God declared His mission statement to Adam and Eve, Satan, and the on-looking universe: "*I will put enmity between thee and the woman, and between thy seed and her seed; it shall bruise thy head, and thou shalt bruise his heel*" (Gen 3:15 KJV).

This prophetic declaration made possible at least two major accomplishments: (1) the planting of a seed of resistance (enmity) in the heart of man so that he would not be under the complete dominion of Satan, and (2) a guarantee of the success of the mission enterprise through the prophetic Seed of the woman (Jesus Christ). Ellen White declares that left to itself, the human race would have formed an alliance with the devil to lead a rebellion against the God of heaven. However, in His infinite wisdom, mercy, and love, God especially interposed to thwart the plan of the devil, so that man, through cooperation with God, could successfully resist the sophistries of the evil one.[5] This was a miracle of divine grace through which God was going to foil the plan of Satan. She further explains, "it is the grace that Christ implants in the soul which creates in man enmity against Satan. Without this converting grace and renewing power, man would continue to be the captive of Satan, a servant ever ready to do his bidding. But the new principle in the soul creates conflict where hitherto had been peace."[6]

In His mercy and love, God was preparing the soil of the human soul so that the prophetic "Seed of the woman" could take root and bear fruit to His honor and glory. In the Seed of the woman was the foreshadowing of a long history of resistance against the hosts of darkness, as the redemptive purpose of God advanced in the earth. From righteous Abel to faithful Noah, the early patriarchs kept faith and hope alive as they called the attention of the then-known world to the divine purposes of God. Yet, this was not without resistance from the seed of the serpent (the line of human beings who carry out the plans of the evil one). Ellen White revealed, "the murder of Abel was the first example of the enmity that God had declared would exist between the serpent and the seed of the woman—between Satan and his subjects and Christ and His followers. Through man's sin, Satan had gained control of the human race, but Christ would enable them to cast off the yoke. Whenever, through faith in the Lamb of God, a soul renounces the service of sin, Satan's wrath is kindled . . . And wherever there are any who will stand in vindication of the righteousness of the law of God, the same spirit will be manifested against them. It is the spirit that through all the ages has set up the stake and kindled the burning pile for the Disciples of Christ."[7]

The people before the flood resisted the grace of God and His urgent appeal to them to turn from their wicked ways. Their alliance with Satan was so strong that *"every inclination of the thoughts of their hearts was only evil continually"* (Gen 6:5 NRSV). To save His mission enterprise, God had to make the painful decision to destroy these antediluvians and preserve a remnant, in Noah and his family, to continue His redemptive purpose in the earth.

The next great revelation of the *Missio Dei* was at the call of Abraham. The Lord said: "Go from your country, you and your kindred and your father's house, to the land that I will show you. I will make of you a great nation, and I will bless you, and make your name great, so that you will be a blessing. I will bless those who bless you, and the one who curses you I will curse; *and in you all the families of the earth shall be blessed."* (Gen 12:1-3, italics mine). As with Adam and Eve in the Garden of Eden, so now with His servant Abraham, God made His intentions extremely clear. He was going to make Abraham the father of a great nation, and through his line the Redeemer of the world would come to be a blessing to all the families of earth.[8] The call of Abraham gave birth to the nation Israel, which became the repository of God's truth and channel of grace to the world. It was God's purpose, through Israel, to expand and extend His redemptive mission to the ends of the earth. His plan was to multiply them, bless them, and produce the long-awaited

SAVING THE LOST: GOD'S MISSION, NOT OURS

Seed of the woman (the Messiah) through them, so that redemptive healing grace would flow in copious measures to lost sinners. However, Israel took all the blessings of God and appropriated them only to itself. Their cherished position as the chosen people of God filled the Jewish nation with boastful pride, blind bigotry, and self-righteous exclusivism. The rich resource of truth, given them to bless the world, became a polluted reservoir of rituals and ceremonies that erected hedges around the way of salvation by placing heavy, meaningless burdens upon the seekers after God.

However, when the Seed of the woman (the Messiah) came, He stripped away the husk of human traditions and pharisaical teachings and recovered the sweet kernel of the everlasting gospel of the Kingdom. Christ came not only as an extension of the *Missio Dei*, but also as the only Guarantee of its success. He came to restore God's mission to its rightful place and to enlist the service of men to help carry out this Divine objective. Jesus' vision of God's mission was very clear. He said: *"The Spirit of the Lord is upon me, because he has anointed me to bring good news to the poor. He has sent me to proclaim release to the captives and recovery of sight of the blind, to let the oppressed go free, to proclaim the year of the Lord's favor"* (Luke 4:18, 19 NRSV). His mission statement was very simple: *"For the Son of Man came to seek out and to save the lost"* (Luke 19:10 NRSV).

Jesus realized that in order for the *Missio Dei* to survive and accomplish its divine objective, He could not work within the established Jewish system of religion. The

Jews' mission agenda did not extend to people beyond the racial and ethnic boundaries of Judaism, and offered preferential treatment to certain classes within Israel. On the other hand, God's mission agenda was all-embracing and all-inclusive, with an open invitation to all human beings. In order to correctly represent the God of mission, Christ had to break ties with the mission traditions of God's chosen people, Israel. Therefore, immediately after His baptism (symbolic anointing) and victory over the Tempter, He went about the task of setting up His Church of called-out believers (Gr. *ekklesia*) as God's final mission agency to the world.

It was not coincidental that the first candidates for Jesus' kingdom campaign were fishermen, for somehow, the vocalizing of the word that described their trade gave added focus to the main objective of Christ's mission. After all, Christ came to seek and to save the lost, and it was in this context that He used the trade name of His first disciples to enlist them as missionaries for the Kingdom of God. His words to them were: "*Follow me, and I will make you fishers of men*" (Matt 4:18 KJV). Thus, Christ gave the word new meaning and elevated it to the noblest task in the world. The first disciples of Jesus were mere *fishers of fish*, but when they met and linked themselves with the Master, He transformed and elevated them to the honorable task of fishing for men.

In like manner, the Savior invites all who are fishing for the transient, mundane things of this life, to link their energies, resources and talents with Him in the most rewarding task of saving lost humanity. Consequently, the call of the church (Gr. *ekklesia*) to participate in the *Missio Dei* is a call to fish for souls, to find people wherever they are and win them for the Kingdom of God. George Eldon Ladd explains that "when Christ had accomplished His redemptive work of death and resurrection, the divine purpose in history moved from Israel, who rejected the Gospel, to the Church—the fellowship of both Jews and Gentiles who accepted the Gospel . . . The Church is 'a chosen race, a royal priesthood, a holy nation' (1 Peter 2:9); and it is through the present mission of the Church, as it carries the Good News of the Kingdom of God unto all the world, that the redemptive purpose of God in history is being worked out."[9]

Where Israel failed in fulfilling its divine charge to extend the Kingdom of God in the world, God expects the church, built upon the Rock (His Son and Our Savior, Jesus Christ), to prevail against the kingdom of darkness and to accomplish His redemptive purpose in the earth. The divine mandate for the church of Christ is very clear: "*All authority in heaven and on earth has been given to me. Go therefore and **make disciples** of all nations, baptizing them in the name of the Father and of the Son and of the Holy Spirit, and teaching them to obey everything that I have commanded you. And remember, I am with you always, to the end of the age*" (Matt 28:19, 20 NRSV, italics mine).

The primary thrust of Jesus' command is to make disciples of every nation. The going, the baptizing, and the teaching are for this one purpose—that is, disciple-making. The mission of the church, therefore, is not just to generate new members, but "to make disciples,[10] who make disciples, who make disciples."[11] Bill Hull puts it this way: "God's primary plan for the church is for disciples of Jesus to develop other men and women into disciples!"[12] It is also very clear that with Christ's command we have the assurance of His presence and His authority. Yet, it is only as the church engages in Christ's mission enterprise that these gifts are truly realized.

Mission, therefore, is God's enterprise from beginning to end, not ours. Irrespective of her calling, her position in salvation history, or her great accomplishments, the role of the church is solely and completely participatory and not supervisory. Sometimes, however, the pride of our humanity gets in the way and makes us conduct ourselves as though mission is all about us—*our* plans, *our* agendas, *our* accomplishments (organizational or personal); what *we* think, what *we* do, how *we* see the lost, and how *we* relate to them.

Moreover, mission is not about the growth and multiplication of institutions, and the complex structures and policies put in place to run them. These may come as by-products of missionary endeavors, but sometimes, these very elements may detract people from the true meaning and purpose of mission. It would be good for us to be often reminded that mission is all about God, His redemptive purpose, and His continuous saving activity in the world. It is about God extending Himself through humanity to save lost humanity. David Bosch wrote that "mission [may be understood] as being derived from the very nature of God. It [is] thus put into the context of the doctrine of the Trinity, not of ecclesiology or soteriology. The classical doctrine on the *Missio Dei* as God the Father sending the Son, and God the Father and the Son sending the Spirit [is] expanded to include yet another "movement": Father, Son, and Holy Spirit sending the church into the world. . . . *mission is not primarily an activity of the church, but an attribute of God. God is a missionary God.* . . . Mission is thereby seen as a movement from God to the world: the church is viewed as an instrument for that mission. . . . *There is church because there is mission, not vice versa.*"[13] (italics mine)

Such an understanding of mission, writes Guder, moves the subject far beyond the level of program or method. It disallows any understanding of mission that makes it a subtopic of the church. The church's very nature is missionary. Thus, the discussion and understanding of mission must be dealt with when we consider God's actions, purposes, promises, and faithfulness.[14] Consequently, the *Missio Dei* is much bigger than we and all *our* claims, *our* ideas, and *our* plans. Guder unequivocally states that "God cannot be restricted to what has been and is happening in Western cultural Christianity. God's work is universal in its intention and impact, and our task is to grapple theologically with that universality. *Our categories for the discussion of mission will prove, again and again, to be too small* over against the comprehensive nature of God's mission"[15] (italics mine). That mission embraces the whole world of lost people, whom God is desperately trying to save. Scripture declares that God, and no one else, is the Reconciler of all mankind. *"If any man be in Christ he is a new creature; the old things passed away; behold, new things have come. Now all these things are from God, **who reconciled** us to Himself through Christ, and gave us the ministry of reconciliation, namely, that **God was in Christ reconciling the world to Himself**, not counting their trespasses against them, and He has committed to us the word of reconciliation. Therefore, we are ambassadors for Christ, as though God were entreating through us; we beg you on behalf of Christ, be reconciled to God"* (2 Cor. 5:17-20, NASB, emphasis mine).

God has never completely relinquished His mission into the control of human beings. He is much too wise and too compassionate to make such a terrible blunder. However, down through the ages, Divine wisdom has selected individuals and people groups to fulfill special roles in God's overall redemptive purpose. In this regard, God has raised up the Seventh-day Adventist Church to participate in His ongoing redemptive activity. To this church He has given a special message for the end-time and the awesome task of preparing a people for the great and terrible day of the Lord's return. Mission, therefore, is not an option for the church today, it is the *raison d'être*, its reason for existence. The church and its mission, despite their importance, are not ends in themselves, but have always been a means to God's great end—the salvation of lost humanity. Should this fact be lost sight of, the church would be in grave danger of becoming dysfunctional, obsolete, and unprofitable for God's mission and the redemptive needs of lost mankind.

Keeping in mind that mission is totally God's enterprise and not *ours*, we will now proceed to look at our understanding of God's call for us to participate in His redemptive work, and how we have responded to the special role that He has assigned us.

Notes

1. Paul Borthwick, *A Mind for Missions* (Colorado Springs, CO: NavPress, 1987), 23.
2. Ellen White is considered by Seventh-day Adventists to be the Lord's messenger to the church. Her ministry and writings have been a constant authoritative source of comfort, guidance, instruction, and correction for the church, and makes clear that the Bible is the standard by which all teaching and experience must be tested. See Fundamental Belief 17 in *Seventh-day Adventists Believe*. . . (Hagerstown, MD: Review and Herald Publishing Association, 1988).
3. Ellen G. White, Patriarchs and Prophets (Boise, ID: Pacific Press Publishing Association, 1958), 63.
4. Darrell L. Guder, The Continuing Conversion of the Church (Grand Rapids: William B. Eerdmans Publishing Company, 2000), 32.
5. Ellen G. White, *The Great Controversy* (Boise, ID: Pacific Press Publishing Association, 1950), 505.
6. Ibid. 506.
7. White, *Patriarchs and Prophets*, 77.
8. Ibid. 125.
9. George Eldon Ladd, "The Gospel of the Kingdom," in *Perspective on the World Christian Movement: A Reader* (Pasadena, CA: William Carey Library, 1992), A-77.
10. Gk. μαθητησ (pronounce *math-ay-tes*) - means a learner. One who learns by following. One who makes the teachings of his master the basis for his life and conduct.
11. Juan Ortiz, Call to Discipleship (Plainfield, N.J.: Logos International, 1975), 18.
12. Bill Hull, *Jesus Christ Disciple Maker* (Grand Rapids: Fleming H.

Revell, 1990), 10.
13. David Bosch, *Witness to the World* (Atlanta: John Knox Press, 1980), 50-57.
14. Darrell L. Guder, 20.
15. Ibid.

2

REMNANT THEOLOGY AND THE SHAPING OF A MISSION STRATEGY

The doctrine of the remnant[1] is a major theological motif in the Seventh-day Adventist Church—one that forms the cornerstone of the church's identity and self-understanding, and gives force and direction to its mission. Throughout the history of the church, the term *remnant*, or the phrase *remnant church*, has been the definitive, self-proclaimed mark of Seventh-day Adventists. Whenever and wherever new members are incorporated into our fellowship, they are required to express the belief that the Seventh-day Adventist Church is the *remnant* church of Bible prophecy. Jon Dybdahl[2] describes the word remnant as being rooted in Adventist history, Adventist theology, and the Adventist psyche. There is no doubt that the doctrine of the *remnant* is quite pivotal in the life, teachings, and future of our church. In this chapter, I will give a brief historical sketch of the development of our remnant theology and will show how our mission strategy has been molded by our remnant self-understanding.

At the 1980 General Conference session held in Dallas, Texas, the Seventh-day Adventist Church officially laid claim to the title of the "remnant," who keep all God's commandments and the faith of Jesus. This claim was expressed as one of the church's twenty-seven fundamental beliefs in the following terms: "The universal church is composed of all who truly believe in Christ, but in the last days, a time of widespread apostasy, a remnant has been called out to keep the commandments of God and the faith of Jesus. This remnant announces the arrival of the judgment hour, proclaims salvation through Christ, and heralds the approach of His second advent. This proclamation is symbolized by the three angels of Revelation 14; it coincides with the work of judgment in heaven and results in a work of repentance and reform on the earth. Every believer is called to have a personal part in this worldwide witness."[3]

It is very important to note, however, that the term *remnant* has been with the Seventh-day Adventist Church long before the official pronouncement of 1980. From their early beginnings, Sabbatarian Adventists who survived the disappointment of the Millerite Movement referred to themselves as the "remnant," the "little remnant," the "scattered remnant," the "little flock," or the "scattered flock."[4] In 1846, Ellen White wrote an article titled "To the Remnant Scattered Abroad"[5] to encourage the small band of persecuted believers. This may have been the earliest use of the term.

Later, on another occasion, she made the solemn appeal, "Let all be careful not to make an outcry against the only people who are fulfilling the description given of the remnant people who keep the commandments of God and have faith in Jesus, who are exalting the standard of righteousness in these last days. God has a distinct people, a church on earth, second to none, but superior to all in their facilities to teach the truth, to vindicate the law of God... Let all... be found at last among those who have the patience of the saints, who keep the commandments of God, and have the faith of Jesus."[6]

It would appear that even though the title *remnant* was in common usage among the battered group of leftover Millerites, Joseph Bates was among the first Sabbatarians to use Revelation 12:17 to apply the title to Adventists. He said, "John saw in vision, that the remnant, [the last end] the Disciples of Christ were persecuted by the dragon for 'keeping the commandments of God, and the testimony of Jesus Christ—Revelation xii: 17.' Now mark! 1. These are the last portions of God's people, and they are keeping His *law*. 2. They are the disciples of Jesus, because they keep His 'testimony'."[7]

However, this connection did not occur as an isolated event, but grew out of an investigative climate in which a number of other theological truths were being hammered out from Scripture as Sabbatarian Adventists sought to develop their own self-understanding and role in salvation history. Pivotal among these truths was a broadening in understanding of the three angels' messages (Revelation 14:6-12), the ministry of Jesus in the heavenly sanctuary (Daniel 8 and 9), the Laodicean call for revival and reformation (Revelation 3:14-22), and the call of God's people out of Babylon (Revelation 17:5 and 18:1-4). It was the understanding of these major bodies of truths that formed the theological framework for Adventist missions.

The early believers saw and understood the connection between the three angels' messages of Revelation 14 and considered themselves God's remnant people, appointed by Him to give His final call to a perishing world. It was around this time (1850's) that Ellen White made the observation that "the three angels' messages formed a 'perfect chain of truth' and that non-Adventists would embrace them in their order, and follow Jesus by faith into the heavenly sanctuary. These messages were represented to me as an anchor to hold the body."[8] Joseph Waggoner and Uriah Smith made similar connections between the Third Angel's Message (which embraces all three messages of Revelation 14), the Laodicean message, and the remnant. According to Smith, "the Third Angel's Message is the final message of mercy to a rebellious world, and the Laodicean message is the final message to a lukewarm church."[9] Writing to Smith a few weeks later, Waggoner said: "The last warning to the world is the Third Angel's Message, and the last admonition to the church is the letter to the Laodiceans."[10]

As all these truths began to fit into one another, the Laodicean message became the rallying point for Adventist mission. This message functioned as a criterion for self-evaluation in the face of the lethargic, but triumphalistic spirit that characterized the Sabbatarian Adventists. In addressing the spirit of the time, James White made it emphatically clear that "our positions are fully sustained by an overwhelming amount of direct scriptural testimony . . . But we, as a people, have evidently rested down upon a theory of truth, and have neglected to seek Bible humility, Bible patience, Bible self-denial, and Bible watchfulness, and sacrifice, Bible holiness, and the power and gifts of the Holy Ghost.... Hence it is said, '*And knowest not that thou art wretched, and miserable, and poor, and blind, and naked*' (Revelation 3:17). What a condition!"[11] One can only wonder what James White would say of the present spiritual condition of the same people today.

In another setting, James White referred to the Laodicean message of Revelation 3:14-22 as a special call to the remnant, directing the attention of believers to a work of preparation for the imminent judgment of the living, so that their sins would be blotted out before the completion of Christ's sanctuary ministry.[12] He also stated that the church had to be stripped of its self-righteous views and feelings and experience true repentance. He denounced the then-current attitude as hypocritical, for in living with the expectancy of the imminent Second Advent and God's judgments on those who disobeyed the Third Angel's Message, "professed believers rushed on in their worldly pursuits, taking their entire energies in pursuit of this world as if there was no coming Jesus, no wrath of God to fall upon the shelterless, and no flaming Judgment-bar, where all deeds will receive a recompense."[13]

It was stirring statements such as this one from the Whites and other stalwart leaders of that day that created the climate and set the tone for Adventist mission. According to P. Gerard Damsteegt, it was this keen self-awareness, facilitated by the pointed testimony of the Laodicean message, that brought about a shift in Adventists' ecclesiological self-understanding from a triumphalistic to an anti-triumphalistic attitude, and provided a powerful incentive to awaken believers to participate in missionary activity even today.[14]

Another element that factored into Adventist understanding of the remnant and its mission was the attitude of the early believers to other religious organizations. In the year preceding the "great disappointment," there arose a surging wave of anti-Millerite sentiments in many of the mainline Protestant churches that were seriously offended by the vociferous end-time proclamations of the Advent movement. These mainline churches began a wholesale disfellowshiping of the Millerites for their "strange" beliefs, and it was not long before leaders in the movement began to associate Protestantism with Roman Catholicism, characterizing them as Babylon.

Foremost among those who were disfellowshiped was Charles Fitch. It was his sermon, *Come Out of Her, My People*, that set the pace for the development of a Babylon theology, which also became a very vocal part of the movement's mission theology. At the Second Advent Conference in Boston (January 28, 1844), William Miller is said to have made the following comment regarding the mother harlot and her daughter in Revelation 17: "If the Roman church was the mother of harlots, then her daughters must be the harlots: and therefore that portion of the

Protestant churches that imitate and partake of the spirit of the old mother must be the daughters referred to."[15]

This view was refined by Joseph Marsh, editor of the Millerite periodical the *Voice of Truth*, as follows: "There can be no question but that the 'woman' is symbolical of the *church*, and as she is called *Babylon*, there can be no dispute but that the church is Babylon. What church? We can make no distinction no farther than the figure will justify. It is a *mother* and her *daughters*—a family of harlots [Revelation 17:5]. We readily admit that the *mother* represents the Catholic Church the eldest member of the family; and we believe her *daughters* symbolize the Protestant sects. If they do not, pray what do they represent? . . . We can see no resemblance between the '*mother,*' a *unit,* and a '*great city* [Revelation 17:18].' But the 'whole family' most strictly represents that city. Take the whole and the figure is perfect; leave out the *children* and it is imperfect."[16]

A few years earlier, in a letter written to Enoch Jacobs, a former Methodist minister and editor of the Day Star, James White made reference to the "organized churches," labeling them as Babylon.[17] Organized religion became a real sore point of dispute for early Adventists. These believers were determined to put as much distance as they possibly could between themselves and the "system of Babylon" because they saw and experienced some of the evils meted out by main-line Protestant denominations. However, because of the rapid growth in membership among Sabbatarian Adventists, the leaders in the movement saw the necessity of bringing more order and organization to the work. This they eventually did, after much debate, at the Battle Creek Conference of Sabbatarian Adventists in 1860, where they chose the name Seventh-day Adventist.

Nevertheless, the leaders and members were very careful and painstaking in their efforts to carve out an "identity" for the new church that was clearly distinct in faith and practice from the mainline Protestant churches from which they came. As a matter of fact, Ellen White saw the name as "a standing rebuke to the Protestant world."[18] Commenting on its missionary significance, she wrote: "The name Seventh-day Adventists carries the true features of our faith in front and will convict the inquiring mind. Like an arrow from the Lord's quiver it will wound the transgressor of God's law, and will lead to repentance toward God, and faith in our Lord Jesus Christ."[19]

When all these historical events and theological arguments are put together, it is not difficult to see why early Adventists took their unpopular position in Protestantism as God's remnant people, those appointed by Him to declare the Third Angel's Message as His final merciful call to earth's inhabitants. Although this claim to "remnancy" sets Seventh-day Adventists in a position over and against their Protestant neighbors, this self-understanding was instrumental in giving impetus and direction to Adventist mission from the time of its adoption in the middle 1800's to today. In the ensuing chapter we shall examine some of the assumptions that underlie our claim to "remnancy" and show how these assumptions influence the mission practice of the church.

Notes

1. The Bible portrays the remnant as a small group of God's people who, through calamities, wars, and apostasy, remain loyal to God. This faithful remnant was the rootstock God used to propagate His visible church on earth. *Seventh-day Adventists Believe: A Biblical Exposition of 27 Fundamental Doctrines* (Washington, DC: General Conference of SDAs, 1988), 161.
2. Jon Dybdahl, "It's God's Call B What It Means To Be The Remnant," Adventist Review 173 (May 9, 1996): 508-510.
3. Ibid. 152.
4. P. Gerard Damsteegt, *Foundations of the Seventh-day Adventist Message and Mission* (Grand Rapids: William B. Eerdmans Pub. Co., 1977), 147.
5. Ellen White, "To the Remnant Scattered Abroad," *Broadside*, April 6, 1846.
6. Ellen White, *The Remnant Church* (Mountain View, CA: Pacific Press Publishing Association, 1950), 46.
7. Joseph Bates, *A Seal of the Living God* (New Bedford, MA: N.p., 1849), 55.
8. Ellen G. White, *Spiritual Gifts*, Vol. 1 (Washington, DC: Review and Herald Publishing Association, 1945), 165-166.
9. Uriah Smith, "The Last Way-Marks," Review and Herald, December 11, 1856, 44.
10. Joseph Waggoner to Uriah Smith, *Review and Herald*, December 25, 1856, 61.
11. James White, "The Seven Churches," *Review and Herald* (October 16, 1856), 189.
12. James White, "The Judgment," *Review and Herald* (January 29, 1857), 100-101.
13. James White, "The Laodicean Church," quoted in P. Gerard Damsteegt, *Foundations of the Seventh-day Adventist Message and Mission* (Grand Rapids:William B. Eerdmans Publishing Company, 1977), 246.
14. Damsteegt, 245.
15. Editorial, "The Conference," *Advent Herald* (February 14, 1844), 9, quoted in P. Gerard Damsteegt, *Foundations of the Seventh-day Adventist Message and Mission* (Grand Rapids: William B. Eerdmans Publishing Company, 1977), 81.

16. Joseph Marsh, "Babylon," p. 128, quoted by James White, ed., *Review and Herald* (December 9, 1851), 58.
17. James White to Enoch Jacobs, Day Star September 20, 1845, 26.
18. Ellen G. White, *Testimonies for the Church*, Vol. 1 (Mountain View, CA: Pacific Press Publishing Association, 1948), 223.
19. Ibid. 224.

3

GOD'S MISSION AND THE REMNANT MIND-SET

*T*he doctrine of the remnant in Adventist theology does not only form the bedrock of our self-understanding and the basis of our mission offensive, but has also played a major role in the creation of a mind-set and social culture that are uniquely Adventist. This mind-set is characterized by a great deal of confidence and assurance in our prophetic origin, our identity as God's remnant, our strong Biblical positions on doctrine, and our definitive understanding of last day events.[1] However, it is this same confident assurance that has shored up the typical weakness of the human nature. This weakness seeks for pre-eminence and self-exaltation, and has manifested itself among us in what I see as four significant dispositions—denominational superiority, people blindness, "us-against-them" mentality, and message above people. This quadruple mind-set has subtly erected stones of stumbling to the church's mission in the world. In this chapter I will simply explore these dispositions that characterize the typical Adventist mind-set and illustrate how they impact on our mission enterprise in the real world.

Denominational Superiority

Seventh-day Adventists, in general, take great pride in the Adventist message,[2] and will not hide or hesitate to show it. Great confidence abounds in our outstanding claim as God's remnant people, with a special message for this end-time generation. However, it is our confidence in strength of this message, and the pride of our claim to "remnancy," that often give a characteristic air of denominational superiority to many Adventist believers. Relying on our remnant theology, many of our members unwittingly (and very often, knowingly) behave as though we are God's favorites, and that all truth proceeds from us and through us, or it is no truth at all. Denominational bias prevails from authors of religious literature, to who is selling the vegetarian food; from who is singing at the concert to which church is sponsoring the community program. If it is not Adventist, the tendency is to reject or ignore it. For example, a church member who receives an invitation in the mail to attend a health lecture may want to verify the denomination of the presenter before deciding to attend. When that member discovers that the presenter is not an Adventist, the typical response is a decision not to attend the lecture.

Among us there is also the practice of defining our church as doctrinally unique and superior to all other Protestant denominations, or as "in opposition to other churches."[3] While there is no disputing our strong doctrinal position, nor room for making apologies for the same, we must be sensitive with respect to our relations to those we regard as unbelievers. However, any ostensible claim or superior stance places the church on the defensive, forcing it to exist in a dynamic tension of trying to preserve a unique identity in the turbulent currents of a secular[4], postmodern[5] culture. As a result, a considerable amount of energy and resources are expended in endeavoring to avoid the negative labeling of being "bigoted," "narrow-minded," "presumptuous," and "fanatical." Since perception appears as reality to the observer, we have every reason to be concerned about the type of triumphalistic[6] image our claim to "remnancy" creates in the minds of other Protestants, and especially secular, post-modern thinkers.

There is near zero tolerance in the post-modern mind-set towards any church that makes such a bold, authoritative claim as we do. While our claims to the truth may be a very important facet of our Adventist image and can be intellectually validated by persuasive Biblical arguments, it may also pose one of our greatest challenges in our efforts to engage and win a postmodern world for the kingdom of God. Stanley Grenz states, "the postmodern mind refuses to limit truth to its rational dimension and thus dethrones the human intellect as the arbiter of truth. There are other valid paths to knowledge besides reason, say the postmoderns, including the emotions and the intuition . . . Knowledge cannot be merely objective, say postmoderns, because the universe is not mechanistic and dualistic but rather historical, relational, and personal. The world is not simply an objective given that is 'out there,' waiting to be discovered and known; reality is relative, indeterminate, and participatory."[7]

Jon Paulien seems pretty much in agreement with this position when he writes, "secular people do not come to faith as a result of intellectual argument but because of an encounter with the living God. And when God has become real to them, their objections usually fall away in light of their new perspective on life."[8] What this means for us as Seventh-day Adventists is that any arrogant, confrontational claim to, or presentation of, the truth for these last days could be met with resistance and ridicule by this postmodern generation. Thus, it becomes critically important that if we are to successfully engage and win this generation for Christ, who is the ultimate truth (John 14:6), a mind-set of denominational arrogance is certainly not the best disposition for us to do the job.

Another reflection of our denominationally superior mentality can be clearly seen in the condescending stance our members, and sometimes church leaders, take toward the teaching and preaching of other Christian denominations. Sometimes we are not very careful regarding the type of comments we make about the doctrinal beliefs and practices of other denominations, especially when we are on the evangelistic warpath. In an effort to make our theological claims stand out, or look superior to those of other denominations, some of our leaders resort to "religious" sarcasm or derogation. I recently observed one of our preachers on public television making really trifling remarks about the teaching and practice of certain Protestant communities. Such behavior, besides being un-Christlike, does not only undermine any opportunity for our members to forge meaningful relationships with people of other faiths, but also sets them up to follow the pastor's cue that this is an acceptable practice.

In addition, we are prone to approach people of other religions with a teaching posture and seldom, if at all, as learners. We often carry a characteristic air of superiority when we are invited to engage in Christian dialogue with members of other denominations, and even though we may not openly say that we are better, our language and posture often betray our claim. This arrogant demeanor serves to hurt our Christian witness and to alienate us from the rest of the Christian community. As a result, we unwittingly erect walls between us and the very ones we are trying to reach with our message.

Sometimes it is rather difficult, almost impossible, for our members to accept invitations to attend church services of other denominations. Very often, these members will not hesitate to express the following: "We are not going to visit your church, because you folks don't have or teach the truth." The idea being conveyed is simply, "We have the truth; you don't." "You need to come to us, but we cannot stoop to come to you." Some of our dear brothers and sisters operate with the notion that they would be violating their consciences to fellowship with "unbelievers." Still others hold to the idea that such "compromise" will be an unholy violation of some unwritten church rule or membership expectation.

May I hasten to say at this point that I am not advocating that, as Seventh-day Adventists, we should habitually seek out the fellowship of non-Adventist congregations. Such a position could be doctrinally hazardous to one's faith, and could unwittingly have the reverse effect of undermining the effectiveness of our witness to members of those congregations. At the same time, however, our members should not feel a burden of guilt or be treated with any defamation or criticism (by members of their local congregation) if they elect to accept an invitation from a friend of another religious community. The basic idea is that we should seek to build bridges to people of other faiths instead of erecting dividing walls.

During her lunch break on the job, my wife was reading a devotional book written by a non-Adventist author. A fellow-worker stopped by and asked my wife about the nature of her reading. After showing the inquirer the cover and title of the book, my wife told her co-worker about its very practical and useful contents. With a little squint in her eyes the co-worker immediately asked: "Is this an Adventist book?" When my wife said that it was not, the woman said: "Good, then I will get one for my sister." During the ensuing discussion, my wife discovered that her co-worker was a victim of Adventist arrogance and religious put-downs and consequently tried to avoid anything related to Seventh-day Adventists. Christ did not call us to erect walls of separation between the rest of the world and ourselves, but to build bridges of love to link the lost world to Him.

Three lurking dangers are readily apparent in this denominational mind-set: *First*, it fosters an environment that produces a false sense of redemptive security—that is, one in which security in Christ is subtly replaced by an over-abiding confidence in the unique calling and message of the Church. Jon Dybdahl has correctly stated, "if there is anything that the history of the remnant concept should teach us, it is the idea that remaining exactly as we are now is dangerous. At one time both Israel and the church in general were the remnant people. That 'remnantness' became lost. Remnantness means being open to truth, being open to continual seeking."[9]

Second, this mind-set can and has produced behaviors that conflict with the servant-leadership model of Christ, our ONLY true example. Ours should not be a position of superiority but one of servant-hood. *Third*, this mind-set can create a misguided perception of the intended target of God's end-time message. Because of our tendency to measure ourselves with the world, we stand in serious danger of missing God's point, that *the message* He has graciously given us to take to the world is also the very *message* by which He intends to *reform* His church. Ellen White says, "the gospel we present for the saving of souls must be the gospel by which our own souls are saved."[10] The Word of God is a quick and powerful two-edged sword[11] that will cut through the hidden thoughts and the intentions of both the messenger and the targeted audience.

We must never forget that God's overall purpose in giving His special end-time message to this church is to prepare a people—not just the world, but also the church—for the great and terrible day of His Divine visitation. We would do well, therefore, to follow the watchful wisdom of the apostle Paul who said: *"I buffet my body and make it my slave, lest possibly, after I have preached to others, I myself should be disqualified"* (1 Corinthians 9:27 NASB).

People Blindness

Another major characteristic of the Adventist mindset as it relates to the mission of the church is that the missionary training given to ministers and members alike predisposes them to be people-blind. Because our ministers and members have been historically trained to witness to Christians of other denominations, they tend to overlook or to shy away from people of non-Christian religions and the unchurched. This aspect of our people-blindness has been reinforced by our sometimes-lopsided presentation of the everlasting gospel, which we often reduce to the Third Angel's Message. The very nature of this message tends to focus our attention upon the spiritual and moral apostasy of modern Christianity. Thus, our evangelistic thrusts seem primarily to zero in on "Mystery Babylon the Great, the Mother of Harlots," and her daughters,[12] to the exclusion of the rest of the un-Christian world. It is also quite possible that we instinctively focus on this aspect of the everlasting gospel—that is, the "Third Angel's Message"—for at least four reasons: (1) it presents God's final message of warning to a lost world; (2) it brings into view some of our major denominational distinctives (the sanctuary and judgment, and the Sabbath); (3) it pinpoints us as the remnant; and (believe it or not) (4) it feeds our denominational pride by showing up the weaknesses and the apostasy of Babylon.

However, the Third Angel's Message represents only one sector of the everlasting gospel and does not resonate with a biblically illiterate, secular world. Hence the secular and unchurched masses of our present societies are completely ignored or overlooked when we do evangelism only in the context of the Third Angel's Message. Over the years, we have baptized scores of Christians from other denominations and have boasted of our vigorous membership accession rate, but nothing, or extremely little, is said of our success rate among non-Christians, or the unchurched, secular world.

Dr. Bert B. Beach, Director of Inter-church Relations for the Adventist World Church, readily confirms, "Adventists have been most successful in reaching religious or semi-religious people, especially those who are already Christians or influenced by Christianity. They have much greater difficulty in reaching secular people or those of other faiths."[13] This phenomenon gives the unwitting impression that the church's task is to point out the error of, and win over, Christians from other denominations, but at the same time, leave the conversion of the non-religious and unchurched to them.

As a direct result of this approach to mission evangelism, the church has been struggling for many years to vindicate itself from the stigma and negative feedback of being labeled "sheep-stealers" and "proselyters." At the 2000 quinquennial session of the General Conference, the world church leaders voted the following statement in an effort to distance the church from any and all visage of proselytism. The article said, "in the context of the dissemination of religion, the issue of 'proselytism' has arisen because the term 'proselytism' is defined in a number of ways and increasingly is being given a pejorative connotation, associated with unethical means of persuasion, including force. Seventh-day Adventists unequivocally condemn the use of such methods. They believe that faith and religion are best disseminated when convictions are manifested and taught with humility and respect, and the witness of one's life is in harmony with the message announced, evoking a free and joyous acceptance by those being evangelized."[14]

The other side of our people-blindness has to do with the way we view and relate to *"non-Christians"* and the unchurched masses of the world. The word non-Christian is italicized because in the Adventist world-view this word has different shades of meaning depending on the audience. However, the tendency among us is to view the world and the people in it through the peculiarities of our Adventist belief system and lifestyle.

Through our Adventist mind-filters we instinctively avoid, or see beyond, people who appear different from us and whose lifestyle is diametrically opposite to ours. If a man or woman is adorned with jewelry, especially if it is worn in "strange places,"[15] the typical assumption of the Adventist mind-set is that this person is not a Christian and does not form a part of our association or circle of friends. People with "strange" hairstyles, tattooed skin, or colored lips are filtered by our mind-set and are seldom beneficiaries of any meaningful Adventist contact, except probably in an evangelistic context. In practice, we do not view these people as promising Christian prospects, and seldom initiate contact with them. However, as fate would have it, sometimes, many of these very "strange" people surprise us by visiting our churches and evangelistic meetings or by suddenly expressing their interest in our lifestyle or message. That is when we take off our filters and start warming up to them with the hope of winning them to our faith.

"Us Against Them"

An unspoken, but very real, component of the typical Adventist mind-set is the "us-against-them" mentality that characterizes the church's mission strategy, and its relationship to people of other religious persuasions. Partnership in mission with other Christian denominations is generally not an option for us, and appears as one of the unspoken rules of conduct for minister and members alike. Church leaders take great pains to ensure that Adventist labeling is attached to all church projects in the community or that the church is highly visible if interdenominational support is needed for any community enterprise. This stance has sometimes hurt the witness of the church and has often been met with hostility and sharp criticism from the leaders and people of other denominations.

While working as a pastor in one of the Caribbean islands in 1989, a team of Adventist ministers (including myself) approached the island's government, requesting the use of one of its abandoned factory sheds to store our disaster relief supplies, in the wake of the tropical hurricane that devastated the island. We were advised that since the availability of such sheds was limited, it would be best that we pool our resources with those of the other local churches and use the shed as a common distribution center for the people of the island. Embarrassingly, we turned down the offer because our administrative leaders and some local church officials would not endorse any joint-relief venture with people of other religious faiths. Instead, our Conference elected to erect our own storage shed for the distribution of our relief supplies to the people of the community. Needless to say, the local government minister was not only disappointed, but pretty upset at the religious narrowness and shallow thinking of our leaders in a time of crisis.

It would appear that the church was more interested in attaching Adventist labels to its humanitarian work for future evangelistic and Harvest Ingathering campaigns, than it was in demonstrating disinterested benevolence to traumatized, needy people. Sometimes, in order to maintain or project our unique "identity" over and against the identity of our Protestant neighbors, we go to religious extremes that benefit neither the cause of Christ nor the church.

At the Adventist World Session 2000 in Toronto, Canada, the church released an official statement that confirmed my observations regarding prevailing mind-sets among Seventh-day Adventists. The statement was aimed at rectifying these negative denominational images and sore-spots, in order to give the church a greater competitive edge and the capacity to generate a more positive and powerful witness in modern society. The official announcement said, "Evangelistic and missionary activity needs to respect the dignity of all human beings. Individuals need to be truthful and transparent when dealing with other religious groups. Terminology should be used which avoids offending other religious communities. Statements that are false or ridicule other religions should not be made. Conversion is an experience of the Spirit, and should therefore in no way be connected to offering and receiving material inducements. While the right to engage in humanitarian activities must be fully recognized, such action must never be linked to evangelism in a way that exploits vulnerable people by offering financial and material incentives to entice them to change religion. Seventh-day Adventists are committed to serving their fellow men by preaching the everlasting gospel to every nation, and kindred, and tongue, and people (Rev 14:6)."[16]

In confirmation of the prevailing us-against-them

mentality among our people, and in the wake of the above statement, Dr. Beach said, "in some locations, churches base their identity on their opposition to other churches."[17] He and other world leaders expressed the hope that there would be a change in the mission and evangelistic philosophy by our churches in those parts of the world. At the press conference, John Graz, Secretary General of the Church's International Religious Liberty Association, said: "As Adventists we uphold the principle that all human beings have the right to choose their religion, or to choose to have no religion. We must accord all humans this basic dignity."[18]

Message Above People

Last, but not least, is the fact that the Adventist concept of mission has created a mind-set among believers that practically elevates the Advent message above communal fellowship and sensitivity to the real needs of real people. A great deal of emphasis is placed on the functional aspect of community life (like lifestyle and behavior, office management, programs, and services), and very little on communal experience (like joyful fellowship, spiritual experience, burden-sharing, and grace-filled community). This has no doubt contributed to the high incidence of apostasy among our ranks. Although many of our former members still believe in the authority and truthfulness of the "Third Angel's Message," some have expressed deep feelings of alienation from the body of Christ.

Here is the example of "David" (not his real name) who became exposed to Adventism during an evangelistic tent crusade. This former member lost his job when he accepted the Sabbath truth and joined our ranks as a committed Seventh-day Adventist Christian. In reflection, he laments over the emotional let-down he experienced after he became a member of the church, on account of the behavior of the same people who were so supportive and encouraging prior to his baptism. He mentioned feeling very alone in his joblessness, and in his search for gainful employment to support his family. What hurt the most, he said, was the cold criticism he received from members when he sought the company of his former friends and tried to get back into his old job. He also resented the fact that many members attribute his leaving the church to his lack of understanding the message and improper indoctrination. David confessed that he understood and still believed in the truthfulness of the Adventist message, but at the time he felt trapped between his economic situation and loyalty to "some people" whose only concern was about getting him into the church and not about really helping him.

Another example is that of "Jenny" (not her real name), a single parent with two children. Jenny was a member of another Protestant denomination before becoming a Seventh-day Adventist. She struggled very long and hard in making her decision to give up the fellowship of her little country church in order to embrace the truth of Adventism. However, after a rather rough initiation into her newly found faith, Jenny went into a spiritual crisis and began missing church services. Needless to say, church members' responses to her situation were mixed—some were supportive and understanding, while others were very critical and cutting. One sister confronted Jenny in the grocery store one day and said to her: "I hope you are not planning to leave the truth." And before Jenny could even reply the sister continued: "When you start missing Sabbath School as you have, the devil will make you backslide right out the church." Jenny later confided that she was too embarrassed and surprised and did not quite know what to say to Sister _____. Not very long after this encounter, Jenny was back in her former church, and nothing I could say to her could convince her to leave. One thing she said to me that I would never forget is that "I love the teaching of the Adventists, but I feel more comfortable in my church."

While doctrinal correctness is very essential in establishing the framework to guide the Christian experience—and we are not lacking in this regard—Christian community and caring concern for the well being of the members of the body are equally essential. As a Christian community, we have fallen short in the latter, and many times our members skirt around this very important issue by appealing to our claim to remnancy, doctrinal uniqueness and peculiar lifestyle. Thus, the church faces a growing challenge in trying to reach people whose Christian walk has been characterized by a high degree of emotional encounter. Often such people are very prone to overlook the doctrinal weaknesses of their denomination—as in the case of Jenny—and are rather unwilling to trade the emotional high they experience in the fellowship of their brethren for what they perceive as the overemphasized, doctrinal correctness, critical judgment, and emotional low of Seventh-day Adventism.

I am afraid that if we continue to focus more on what people should or should not do (message-centeredness and task-orientation) and fail to listen to what is on people's minds, to help them individually and collectively find their way (loving and supportive community), we will be setting the stage for them to become easily discouraged and give up on their fellowship with the church, and often with Christ.

It is not very difficult for anyone to see the Seventh-day Adventist Church as a message-centered organization. The message-centeredness that is spoken of here has nothing to do with our commitment to truth, or staying faithful to Scripture, but with the creation of an internal spiritual climate that gives more preeminence to conformity to a system of beliefs over the reproduction of a loving and caring Christian community. In other words, the message is given preeminence over the needs of real people, and head religion over heart religion. Russell Staples insightfully suggests, "perhaps we should be honest enough to admit that there has been a tendency towards a legalistic judgmentalism within the Adventist community. Precisely because the truth of the message is taken with utter seriousness and because of an apocalyptic view of the judgment, any deviation from truth and moral rectitude may serve as a cause for discipline or correction. This may easily result in a tendency toward a legalistic rather than a grace orientation. And it may also undercut the joyous sense of victory that should fill the Christian's soul."[19]

It is very easy for us to become so entranced by our biblical heritage and captivating message that we altogether lose our perspective on the reason for which both were given. The real goal of our mission is people. The message is a tool for reaching, nurturing, and discipling them. We were not called just to talk about the glorious product that we have, but to get the product to all people, in the world.

It is quite possible that our perception of our end-time calling has created a religious community that is not only task-oriented and message-centered, but organization-centered as well. Everything the church does centers around the message and the life of the organization, making the body of Christ subservient to the instruments that were designed to serve and support it. Alan Andreasen,[20] in his attempt to outline measures to help nonprofit organizations determine and understand their operational focus, has aptly described conditions that are at home within the Seventh-day Adventist church. He suggested that the following are symptoms of a product-oriented organization:[21]

1. <u>Seeing the offering (in the church's case, the message) as inherently desirable</u>. Seventh-day Adventist laity and ministry seldom entertain the thought that the potential prospect may not share their enthusiasm or values about the Advent message. There is the tendency among us

to believe that the uniqueness and truthfulness of the message are sufficient to attract non-members. Pastors and church members sometimes express surprise, often bordering on frustration, whenever there is a poor response (in terms of numbers deciding to join our ranks) to a presentation series of the Adventist message. The feeling expressed is: "The truth was so clear, why aren't these people accepting it? What's wrong with them?" The general expectation appears to be that since we have the best product (in terms of message) in town, people would beat a path to our door. The reality is that we have failed in the area of packaging our product in forms that will appeal to modern society.

2. <u>The notion of community ignorance</u>. Often we tend to ascribe lack of interest in the Advent message to the fact that prospects are either "gospel-hardened" or do not fully understand or appreciate the high standards the message proclaims. There is also the general assumption that believers leave the church because of this lack of understanding due to improper indoctrination—the assumption being that if they really knew this message they never would have left the truth.

3. <u>Overemphasis on programs and promotion</u>. Local church leaders have been schooled in trickle-down program promotion to meet set agendas of the higher organization, which are sometimes quite irrelevant to the local situation of the church. There is always some new program to be promoted, and quite often these programs do not start with the needs of the people they are intended to serve, but with

individual or collective perceptions of church leaders. Thus, pastors and members have become more program-friendly than people-centered. Local church ministry generally takes its departure from a program to be promoted or sold to the congregation, rather than from the perspective of congregational or community needs. Once the program is received from the higher organization, pastors and members spend a lot of time and energy promoting it in order to gain membership acceptance and support. This approach to organizational leadership stifles the creative capacity of the local congregation to develop its own mission paradigm and vision of ministry.

   4. <u>The secondary role of community research</u>. The typical church member assumes that the reason for the lack of interest in the Adventist message is the public's ignorance, and the only solution for the problem is not doing research on people's needs, but a more vigorous and consistent proclamation of the message. There is very little sense of the customers' perspective about us, and if research is done at all, it is mainly pursued to confirm our belief about the population under study. This is what I call "mission myopia"—an approach initiated and sustained by organizational needs and presuppositions, with very little regard for concerns and needs of the mission target. For example, who is the focus of the present style of Adventist evangelism? Is it the "mis-located" Christians in apostate Protestantism, non-Christians, or the un-churched? An honest review of our evangelistic history will reveal that our default target (based on our understanding of the Third

Angel's Message) has always been apostate Protestantism, with the hope that the other groups will fall in by the way.

However, our lack of customer perspective has adversely affected our mission and ministry effectiveness to the church members on the inside, and to non-members on the outside. On the inside, the needs of church volunteers (internal customers) are subservient to preset positions and programs, and on the outside, instead of asking the questions to ascertain peoples' needs, we give answers to questions they are not asking. The Advent message is treated as the generic solution to problems of non-members, who are generally called "unbelievers" (whether they are Christians of other religious persuasions or not), and looked upon as being part of the system of Babylon.

    5. <u>One best marketing strategy</u>. This most certainly applies to our approach to evangelism. Tent crusades, cottage meetings and revelation seminars have become the standing norm for the mission outreach of the local Adventist congregation. In recent times, we have adopted a more glorified form of the same approach by making use of high-tech electronic media. For example, we have simply substituted the laptop computer and PowerPoint presentations for the slide projector. A different technology, but the same one best method—a series of predictable messages in a generic format of intellectual argumentation.

    But what about strategic planning—from mission and ministry development to mission and ministry assessment?[22] What about the empowerment of church members to function in the areas of their giftedness? And what of allowing the needs (spiritual and to a lesser extent social and cultural) of the target audience to inform our approach and the presentation style and format of our message? Even though the intellectual argumentation approach to evangelism seems to appeal to a certain class of people, it may not be the ideal approach for reaching the growing secular, unchristian world. Although the mass marketing approach of net-evangelism may have the benefit of worldwide coverage, it lacks the flexibility to be translated into the context of the culturally diverse audiences.

Andreasen[23] attributes this "one best strategy" approach to administrators' monolithic view of society (people-blindness in our case), caused by their lack of contact with changing societal needs. One best strategy is usually the easiest and fastest to put into action. Since pastoral ministry is generally driven by numbers orchestrated by the local Conference, the tent crusade and revelation seminars have been the typical evangelistic tool of choice, in preference to other approaches which are perceived to be slower and less yielding.

6. <u>Ignoring generic competition</u>. As Seventh-day Adventists, we believe that we hold biblically sound doctrinal beliefs that are indisputable, and because of this we are able to successfully defend our theological positions against challenges presented by those who are not of our faith. However, this sense of confidence has undermined our ability to identify and deal with all the competitive forces that seek to control the souls of human beings. We have a tendency

to rely on the strength of our message and membership loyalty to pull us through difficult times and situations, and often fail to take strategic measures to maintain a position of competitive advantage on earth's multi-complex battlefield. Thus, we operate from a reactive rather than a pro-active position.

There is also the general assumption among us that our competitors are other Christian denominations that hold different systems of beliefs than ours. This assumption appears to be generated by our understanding of our eschatological role in the context of the "Third Angel's Message." Thus, we tend to focus most of our attention on what's going on with apostate Protestantism, with absolutely no meaningful consideration being given to the non-Christian religions, the unchurched, and the fast-growing influences of a secular, postmodern society. Every Sabbath morning and throughout the week, church members are bombarded, through the media and through communal interaction, with many alternatives to sitting down to listen to tame, traditional, predictable preaching.

However, while we remain focused on what the other Christian churches are doing and not doing, the devil is moving through our back-door and securing the interest of our members in his ungodly, diabolical affairs. Maybe as a church we have not done a thorough job in defining who or what is our competition in terms of outreach (targeting the unsaved), and in-reach (membership conservation).

Who and what are we competing against in the battle for souls on the outside, and who and what are we competing against for the conservation of souls on the inside? George Barna insightfully suggests that the church's main competition "is not with other churches—it is with organizations, opportunities, and philosophies that provide people with an alternative to the Christian life. Our main competition is from organizations like ABC, CBS, Universal Studios, MGM, K-Mart, 7-11, JC Penney, and so forth . . . How many local churches do you know that are able to compete with the same tough-mindedness, the same highly focused sense of purpose, and an equivalent level of professionalism in promoting their ministry (line of business) and product offerings (services) as their secular competitors?"[24]

While we may not agree with Barna that other churches do not comprise our competition—because of our view of modern-day Protestantism in the light of apocalyptic eschatology—we must agree, in principle, that our main competition is anything or anyone who can offer people (including our own members) any other lifestyle than the one called "Christian." This understanding of our competition will not only assist us in dealing with the challenges of engaging with fallen Babylon over the souls of men, but also with the educating and preparing of our people to deal with subtle influences of a secular, hedonistic society.

However, it is both troubling and perilous that we appear so confident in our historical and theological positions, and the compelling power of our message, that we worry very little, if at all, about any competition. In other words, "we have need of nothing" (Rev. 3: 17). But present realities indicate that, as a church, we are experiencing unprecedented spiritual inertia due to the competitive forces of secularism which are making serious inroads into the thought processes, lifestyle, and behavior of our people. Secular drift[25] is a present reality for the Seventh-day Adventist church, and we have not been able to adequately address it for the simple reason that we have taught our members to feel safe in the certainty of our Biblical origin and the validity of our doctrine and teachings. However, Jon Paulien depicts the reality that "in a secular world an intellectual faith is no longer sufficient to guard against the secular drift. Adventists, therefore, are crying out more and more for a living walk with God, for a taste of His presence."[26]

I sincerely encourage the teachers and leaders of our people to use their God-given wisdom and energies to remove this false sense of security from among our people, and center their hope and complete reliance, not on our remnant calling or our doctrinal positions, but *solely* on the person and power of Jesus Christ.

Surely, the concept of the remnant is a firm, pivotal anchor-point in Adventist theology. It gives us a valid understanding of a judgment-bound world and a clarion call to proclaim a Christ-centered gospel that announces the imminent return of our Lord. In this context, our claim to remnancy represents our call to a special mission and our indebtedness to the lost world. Therefore, our remnant calling should not be portrayed as a badge of special status.[27] Dybdahl has correctly stated, "being part of the remnant is a life journey of mission, not a sign that we have arrived at a superior status. Our duty is to give the message lovingly and faithfully and let God make final decisions."[28] Moreover, we must never allow our claim to remnancy and strong theological positions to replace the person and the power of Christ as our only source of hope and salvation.

It is very evident that there is an urgent need for modification of the Adventist mind-set if we are to successfully engage our postmodern society with the gospel of Jesus. As I stated earlier, this triumphalistic mind-set is characterized by attitudes and behavior patterns that portray (1) denominational superiority, (2) people blindness, (3) "us-against-them" mentality, and (4) an atmosphere where message has pre-eminence over people. In the next chapter, I will show the flaws in each of these mental dispositions, and use the life and teachings of Christ to demonstrate God's ideals for His people, as they relate to the fulfillment of His mission here on earth.

Notes

1. See P. Gerard Damsteegt, *Foundations of the Seventh-day Adventist Message and Mission*; LeRoy E. Froom, *Prophetic Faith of Our Fathers*; *The Historical Development of Prophetic Interpretation* 4 vols. (Washington, DC: Review and Herald Publishing Association, 1950); Seventh-day Adventists Believe: *A Biblical Exposition of 27 Fundamental Doctrines* (Washington, DC: General Conference of SDAs, 1988); Raoul Dederen, ed. *Handbook of Seventh-Day Adventist Theology* (Hagerstown, MD: Review and Herald Publishing Association, 2000).
2. Adventist message refers to our distinctive doctrines and teachings, such as: the sanctuary and investigative judgement, the Sabbath, the state of the dead, eschatology, spirit of prophecy, 2nd coming, health and temperance, etc.

3. Statement made at the press conferences held after the release of the official announcement of Adventist position on Religious Liberty, Evangelism, and Proselytism was made on July 4, 2000.
4. Secularization describes a process in which religious ideas, values, and institutions lose their public status and influence and eventually even their plausibility in modern society. Craig M. Gray, *The Way of the (Modern) World Or, Why It's Tempting to Live As If God Doesn't Exist* (Grand Rapids: William B. Eerdmans Publishing Company, 1998), 19.
5. According to Stanley J. Grenz, postmodernism refers to an intellectual mood and an array of cultural expressions that call into question the ideals, principles, and values that lay at the heart of the modern mind-set. Stanley Grenz, *A Primer of Postmodernism* (Grand Rapids: William B. Eerdmans Publishing Company, 1996), 12. This mind-set was best summarized by Charles Jencks in his description of the renowned Jürgen Habermas' Enlightenment Project, of which he said: it became the goal of the human intellectual quest to unlock the secrets of the universe in order to master nature for human benefit and create a better world. This quest led to the modernity characteristic of the twentieth century, which sought to bring rational management to life in order to improve human existence through technology. Charles Jencks, *What Is Post-Modernity?* 3rd ed. (New York: St. Martin's Press. 1989), 8.
6. Triumphalism is the doctrine, attitude, or belief that one religious creed is superior to all others. *Merriam-Webster's College Dictorinary (1998), s.v.*
7. Stanley J. Grenz, *A Primer of Postmodernism* (Grand Rapids: William B. Eerdmans Publishing Company, 1996), 7.
8. Jon Paulien, *Present Truth in A Real World* (Boise, ID: Pacific Press Publishing Association, 1993), 10.
9. Jon Dybdahl, "It's God's Call – What It Means to be the Remnant," *Adventist Review* 173 (May 9, 1996):508-510.
10. Ellen White, *Counsels On Sabbath School Work* (Hagerstown, MD: Review and Herald, 1966), 100.
11. Revelation 17:5 KJV. "Babylon the Great" is the name by which Inspiration refers to the great threefold religious union of the papacy, apostate Protestantism, and spiritism. "Babylon the great" includes apostate Protestantism at the time here envisioned. The daughters of this "mother" thus represent the various religious bodies that constitute apostate Protestantism. *The Seventh-day Adventist Bible Commentary* vol. 7 (Hagerstown, MD: Review and Herald Publishing Association, 1980), 852.
12. B. B. Beach, "Adventism and Secularization," *Ministry* (April, 1996): 22.
13. Official Statement on Religious Liberty, Evangelism, and

Proselytism was voted by the General Conference of Seventh-day Adventists Administrative Committee (ADCOM), for release at the time of the General Conference Session in Toronto, Canada, June 29-July 9, 2000.
14. Off the ordinary, bordering bizarre.
15. Official Statement on Religious Liberty, Evangelism, and Proselytism.
16. Statement made at the press conferences held after the release of the official announcement of Adventist position on Religious Liberty, Evangelism, and Proselytism was made on July 4, 2000.
17. Ibid.
18. Russell L. Staples, *Community of Faith* (Hagarstown, MD: Review and Herald Publishing Association, 1999), 66-67.
19. Alan Andreasen, "Nonprofits: Check Your Attention to Customers," *Harvard Business Review* (May-June 1982): 107-109.
20. For Seventh-day Adventism the "product" is its unique system of doctrinal beliefs, teachings, and lifestyle.
21. See chapter six for further development of this idea.
22. Ibid.
23. George Barna, *Marketing the Church: What They Never Taught You About Church Growth* (Colorado Springs, CO: NavPress, 1988), 29.
24. See Jon Paulien, *Present Truth in the Real World* (Boise, ID: Pacific Press Publishing Association, 1993) 53-68, for a full explanation of the "secular drift" and how Adventists become secular.
25. Ibid.
26. Dybdahl, 508-510.
27. Ibid.

4

A MIND-SET FOR GOD'S MISSION

The current mission challenges facing the Seventh-day Adventist Church around the world, and especially in the West, present an urgent need for an ongoing re-examination and re-adjustment of the way we think and do mission and ministry. This does not imply automatic dismantling or abandonment of the traditional approaches of mission evangelism and ministry that have successfully contributed to the growth and development of Adventism since its early beginnings. Some of these methods and forms should remain in order to facilitate the needs of traditional church members who are prone to have great difficulty adjusting to change. However, the church must engage in an ongoing process of careful examination and evaluation of its approaches to mission and ministry in order to make the Advent Movement a more viable mission operation. This re-examination and re-adjustment also infer refining and enhancing the church's organizational structure and mission outlook, for greater efficiency and effectiveness in the pursuit of mission objectives.

Times are changing, and every day brings new challenges, not just to the church as a body, but also to individual members comprising the body. If the church does not make organizational and functional adjustments to meet these challenges of our rapidly changing times, it will not be able to engage in ministries that resonate with the needs of society, and will be ingloriously left behind as an irrelevant source of authority for shaping modern life and thought. Barna writes, "today, organizational survival requires the ability to evaluate the environment, and adapt one's style to keep pace with the changes. Survival does not require compromising one's morals or vision, or the gospel. It does, however, necessitate a clear understanding of the territory within which an individual or organization will attempt to demonstrate those morals and convey that vision."[1]

Kotler and Levy also make this very important statement: "For an organization to remain viable, its management must provide for periodic audits of its objectives, resources, and opportunities. It must reexamine its basic business, target groups, differentiated advantage, communication channels, and messages in the light of current trends and needs."[2] These very timely statements are worthy of our keen consideration as we contemplate the future of Adventist mission around the world. In light of this, I envision the application of *selected principles*[3] of marketing management as excellent managerial tools for overall organizational evaluation and strategic planning. In this context, marketing will not be "about a new way of perceiving the Lord Jesus Christ, but about coping with change, competing against the world's attractive alternatives, and making the gospel responsive to today's seekers. It will involve taking the essentials of the ancient faith and contextualizing them to speak to the needs of modern society."[4]

However, in order to pave the way for implementing a marketing approach to mission and ministry, it is very important to sensitize church leaders and members to the relevance and significance of market-oriented thinking and planning as they relate to organizational mission objectives. To do so, the typical Adventist mind-set, which tends to be triumphal, message-centered, and organization-centered, must be held in abeyance (so to speak), so that church leaders and members may have the opportunity to see the benefits of approaching mission from a different perspective. Instead of doing mission from the *inside out* (focusing primarily on organizational needs and goals), mission will be conducted from the *outside in* (focusing on the needs of the lost and what *must* to be done to save them).[5] With this approach, the primary focus of mission will not be the message or the organization formed to carry it out (even though these are very essential in themselves), but the people whom the church and the entire mission process have been designed to reach. Bill Hybels states, "authentic evangelism flows from a mind-set that acknowledges the ultimate value of people—forgotten people, lost people, wandering people, up-and-outers, down-and-outers—all people. The highest value is to love them, serve them, and reach them. Everything else goes up in smoke."[6] I could not agree more.

Denominational Superiority or Servant Leadership?

Our claim to remnancy has, more often than not, created an un-Christlike disposition of denominational superiority in many of our church members. Traditionally, we posit ourselves as the religious elite and the only bastion of religious truth, categorizing other Christian and non-Christian religious organizations as unbelievers and a part of the system of mystical Babylon.[7] As a direct outgrowth of this religious stance and the subtle inherent human desire for supremacy, there is the tendency among us to look condescendingly on what God might be doing in other religious communities. The attitude most often projected is that, if it does not happen here (within our community of faith), then it is not authentic.

From the pulpit and in the pew, we have learned to discredit, minimize, and sometimes ascribe to the kingdom of darkness, religious activities and supernatural occurrences in non-Adventist congregations. For example, the religious experiences of other Protestants are often held suspect whenever they convert to Seventh-day Adventism. These children of God are sometimes treated as though their walk with God, prior to their embracing the Third Angel's Message, did not count for much. Thus, many are encouraged to be re-baptized as a symbol of their acceptance of the full body of truth as proclaimed by God's Remnant Church.

While our official theology admits that we are not the only true Christians in the world, our un-official theology demonstrates that, in some quarters, one's Christianity is not valid until he or she enters the portals of the Seventh-day Adventist church. What appears to be happening here in these cases is that our unofficial theology is overwhelming our official theological position. According to Millard J. Erickson, "our official theology is what we believe in theory, what we say we subscribe to. . . . Our unofficial theology is what we actually believe in practice, the belief that underlies what we do, and is revealed in our actions."[8]

While our official church position allows for the reception of baptized, practicing Christians from other denominations into its fellowship, based on the profession of their faith in Jesus Christ, there are still some parts of the world church where these new believers are still required to be re-baptized whenever they wish to embrace Adventism. Appealing to Paul's encounter with some disciples of John,[9] in Acts 19, as a justification for their actions, some pastors and evangelists encourage (in some cases demand) re-baptism of Christian non-members, even when these believers were already baptized by immersion in the name of Jesus. This practice, however, raises very serious questions that we need to prayerfully ponder.

What is the real reason behind re-baptizing an individual who is already a believing, practicing Christian? Are we placing more priority on becoming an Adventist via baptism over the work that Christ has already done in the heart of His believing children prior to their encounter with Adventism? Is this a subtle form of boasting that we are better? Are we putting unnecessary hedges before people who simply want to extend their faith and continue their walk with their Lord as He leads them into more truths?

Another manifestation of our air of religious superiority is our pejorative stance toward miracles occurring outside of Adventist circles, especially in the area of healing. Although the working of miracles does not validate doctrinal correctness, or forms the basis for testing the genuineness of one's faith, the general assumption among us is that these miracles are not authentic since such people do not teach or obey the truth as we understand it. However, many of our people forget that Biblical healing is not based on religious orthodoxy—though sound doctrine is good and necessary—but on living faith in God and His Son, Jesus Christ. It is faith in God, not doctrine, which brings healing to the believer. Hence the reason Christ performed many miracles among the Gentiles, while, in many cases, He refused to do the same in Israel. While the Jews relied on their biological, historical and doctrinal heritage for divine favor, their surrounding neighbors had nothing but their faith in the mercy and power of God. It is rather sad to say that many of our believers are making the same mistake as the Jews in Jesus' day.

New Testament figures like the Roman centurion (Luke 7:1-9), the Syrophoenician woman (Matthew 15:21-28), the Samaritan woman at Jacob's well (John 4), Cornelius (Acts 10), and others stand as irrefutable testimonies to the fact that it is not dead orthodoxy that moves the arms of omnipotence, but the steadfast confidence in God's ability and power to act on behalf of those who diligently seek Him. It is rather ironic that while the Jews boasted of having the Abrahamic covenant, the Law of Moses, and the teachings of the prophets they did not have faith in the very One who gave life and meaning to these dead forms. Although these Gentile icons of faith did not share the heritage of their Jewish neighbors, they found life and meaning by trusting and embracing the One the Jews rejected.

Needless to say, the blessings of God upon those living outside the Jewish community always bruised the religious pride of the "favored" people and provoked their envy and jealousy. This was clearly the case with Jesus' disciples in Luke 9:49, 50: "John said to him, 'Teacher, we saw someone casting out demons in your name, and we tried to stop him, because he was not *following us*.' But Jesus said, 'Do not stop him; for no one who does a deed of power in my name will be able soon afterward to speak evil of me. Whoever is not against us is for us' " (NRSV, italics mine).

The point here appears to be rather clear. John seems to be speaking on behalf of his fellow disciples, and articulated the common feelings of the group. Obviously, the disciples felt that they were the privileged followers of the Messiah and the only true recipients of His miraculous power. It is also quite possible that the disciples were filled with jealousy since they were not able to cast the evil spirit out of the boy at the foot of the mountain only a short while prior to this incident (Luke 9:28ff). Apparently, they just could not bear the thought that God would bypass them and credit others with His healing grace. Since Jesus is the same yesterday, today, and forever (Hebrews 13:8), how does our attitude measure up to His approach to others working in His name?

This indeed was the case of the leadership of Israel when the magi, from the East, came to Jerusalem inquiring about the birth of the long-awaited Messiah. Ellen White reveals, "these learned teachers would not stoop to be instructed by those whom they termed heathens. It could not be, they said, that God had passed them by, to communicate with ignorant shepherds or un-circumcised Gentiles."[10] These teachers of Israel believed themselves to be God's chosen channels of truth and revelation, and could not conceive of God stooping so low as to reveal His hidden purpose to the unlearned and the uncircumcised. They thought that they had God all boxed in and figured out, that they alone held the only patent rights on divine grace, but "while God was opening the door to the Gentiles, these Jewish leaders were closing the door to themselves."[11]

This mind-set has some serious implications for us who are living in the end time. Commenting on the Jewish mental framework, Ellen White said, "the Jewish people had been made the depositories of sacred truth; but Pharisaism had made them the most exclusive, the most bigoted, of all the human race. Everything about the priests and rulers–their dress, customs, ceremonies, traditions—made them unfit to be the light of the world. They looked upon themselves, the Jewish nation, as the world. But Christ commissioned His disciples to proclaim a faith and worship that would have in it nothing of caste or country, a faith that would be adapted to all peoples, all nations, all classes of men."[12]

Could it be that we are repeating this sad Jewish history? Could our present attitude toward non-Adventists (Christians and non-Christians) be characterized as Pharisaic and bigoted? Are we fit to be light-bearers to the world? As a last-day movement, called to proclaim a special message of mercy and warning to a soon-to-perish world, could we be projecting, by our attitude and behavior, that we are God's beloved, endowed with His special benefits and privileged favor? In the eyes of the non-Adventist observer, does our religious stance suggest that we alone have the patent rights on the choicest blessings of heaven? Is God stuck with the Seventh-day Adventist Church? Or will He dare work out His purpose through other denominations, organizations, or people? Ellen White clearly reminds us, "Christ recognized no distinction of nationality or rank or creed. The scribes and Pharisees desired to make a *local* and a *national benefit* of all the gifts of heaven and to *exclude the rest of God's family in the world.* But Christ came to break down every wall of partition. He came to show that His gift of mercy and love is as *unconfined* as the air, the light, or the showers of rain that refresh the earth"[13] (italics mine).

God alone is sovereign, and His blessings and benefits flow to whomsoever He wills, for His own purpose and His own glory. This glory He shares with no other—be it principality, power, people-group denomination or organization. This undeniable truth was clearly illustrated in the account of Peter's introduction to the Gentile Cornelius (See Acts 10). It was quite evident that God was already at work outside the Jewish community, for he sent His angel to instruct Cornelius that his prayers and his gifts were accepted by heaven, and that He (God) was going to bring salvation to his household (Acts 10:1-8). The same God who gave Peter the vision to neutralize his Jewish prejudice so that he could reach out to the Gentiles is the same God who gave Cornelius his vision and instruction. Moreover, God confirmed what He was doing outside the Jewish community of faith by the outpouring of His Spirit (Acts 10:44-48). Finally, in his report to the Jewish council, Peter made this very cogent and insightful remark: "If God therefore gave to them [*the Gentiles*] the same gift as He gave to us also after believing in the Lord Jesus Christ, *who was I that I could stand in God's way?*" (Acts 11:17, NASB, italics mine).

Through this remarkable experience of God's presence and blessings upon the Gentiles in the Person of His Spirit, Peter came to understand the universal truth: "I most certainly understand now that God is not one to show partiality, but in *every* nation the *person* who fears Him and does what is right, is welcome to Him." (Acts 10:34, 35 NASB, italics mine). *The God of heaven, and of mission, is not subject to any person, religion, creed, culture, or ethnic group, even those whom He has chosen to carry out His eternal purpose.* It is therefore within reason to conclude that even though God has entrusted us with a special message for these last days, He is, nevertheless, at work among other Christian communities, seeking out and saving those who are honestly seeking Him.

God's dealing with His favored people in the past can give us a fairly accurate idea of what He expects of us in these very crucial moments of earth's history. Paul tells us, in 1 Corinthians 10:11, 12, that Israel's experience as God's chosen people is recorded for our instruction in the end time. Consequently, we need not hold to the idea that we are the only ones favored of God and that non-Adventists are not. No doubt, Adventists believe they have a special message to bear to the world, but this prevailing mind-set of denominational superiority is very much unrepresentative of the Savior who called us into His service, and is therefore unwarranted. We desperately need to embrace God's message that is revealed through His dealing with Peter in Acts 10 and 11, if we are to successfully carry out the mission He has entrusted to us.

What Can We Learn from Israel?

In the book of Romans, chapters 9 through 11, Paul portrays a brief but tragic history of Israel as the chosen people of God. He laments: "I am telling the truth in Christ, I am not lying, my conscience bearing me witness in the Holy Spirit, that I have great sorrow and unceasing grief in my heart. For I could wish that I myself were accursed, *separated* from Christ for the sake of my brethren, my kinsmen according to the flesh, who are Israelites, to whom belong the adoption as sons and the glory and the covenants and the giving of the Law and the *temple* service and promises, whose are the fathers, and from whom is the Christ according to the flesh, who is over all, God blessed forever. Amen" (Rom 9: 1-5 NASB, italics mine).

From the entire scenario that follows this sad introduction, several important points emerge (as discussed hereunder) that are very instructive for us, since we consider ourselves to be fulfilling a role similar to that given to the children of Israel:

1. Election is always for the fulfillment of God's purpose, and is based totally on His grace and mercy, not on human capability, uniqueness, or stellar accomplishments (Rom 9:11-16; Deut 7:6-9; 11:5, 6). So there is absolutely no room for boasting, nor any sense of favoritism, nor any claims of supremacy. According to Christopher Wright, "the calling of Israel to bear faithful witness to the revelation of the living God entrusted to them was not a matter of Israel's flaunting their privilege in an attitude of 'our religion is better than yours'—as if Israel's faith was one among many brands of a commodity, 'human religion'. Rather, what was at stake, what was so threatened by Israel compromising with the gods and worship of other nations, was *the continuity of the redemptive work of the Creator God of all mankind within the unique historical and social context which he himself had chosen*"[14] (italics mine).

In a similar manner we should not be flaunting our historical and doctrinal uniqueness in an attitude of religious superiority and self-congratulation, as though we are called to measure ourselves against other denominations. Our position in history and eschatology is strictly one of undeserved privilege, responsibility, and humble service.

2. Election is always for a purpose—God's purpose and not the purpose or the agenda of the elected (Deut 7:8; Gen 12:1-3; see also 1 Pet 2:9). God has a supreme purpose that transcends times and generations, and He is always working in every situation to produce it. The apostle Paul declares, *"And we know that **all things** work together for good to those who love God, to those who are the called according to **His purpose**. ²⁹ For whom He foreknew, He also **predestined to be conformed to the image of His Son**, that He might be the **firstborn among many brethren**"* (Rom 8:28, 29, NKJV, emphases mine).

From the above scripture we know the God's purpose determines the outcome of everything in every generation. Furthermore, we understand that God has already predetermined what His purpose is—that is, to form the image of Christ in His brethren (all who are born-aging in Him). Consequently, God's purpose or goal is not the Advent message, or even the people proclaiming it; but the Life of the Advent Savior reflected in those who proclaim the Advent message. Therefore, we must not be found guilty of putting denominational agendas above God's purpose of reproducing the image of Christ in every believer.

3. Election is contingent on the fulfillment of God's purpose (Rom 11:7-12). God rejected Israel because they

failed to fulfill the purposes for which they were called and became a stumbling block to the very ones they were called to reach with the good news of the anointed One and Savior of the world. The Jewish leader spent their days promoting the supremacy of their religion instead of preparing their people and the world for the prophesied Redeemer. Are we satisfied that we are fulfilling God's purpose for us as it relates to our mission in this world?

4. God is not stuck with any people—Israel, Seventh-day Adventists, or any other. Salvation history shows that His purpose supersedes earthly establishments or organizational agendas, and His will shall be done on earth as it is in heaven, with or without the people He has chosen to help accomplish it (Rom 11:17-26). God is never short on options, and He will always find a way to fulfill His purpose. To the Jewish leaders and people who were prone to think that God was stuck with them, John the Baptist said: "You brood of vipers, who warned you to flee from the wrath to come? Therefore bring forth fruits in keeping with repentance, and do not begin to say to yourselves, we have Abraham for our father, for I say to you that God is able from these stones to raise up children to Abraham" (Luke 3:7-8 NASB).

In the economy of heaven, there is absolutely no room for pedestal mentality or "better-than-thou" attitude. God bestows His special favor upon individuals so that they can use His blessing to serve others, not lord it over them. "From everyone to whom much is given, much will be required" (Luke 12:48 NRSV), and we need to be extremely prayerful (not boastful) here. Our special position in salvation history has nothing to do with an inherent value in us as a people, but everything to do with God's mercy and grace and with the sacred task to which He has called us.

In the message to Laodicea,[15] which we have traditionally applied to ourselves,[16] the True and Witness bears straight and pointed testimony that challenges every visage of denominational supremacy, bigotry, self-sufficiency, and exclusivity. Ellen White says: "Here is represented a people who pride themselves in their possession of spiritual knowledge and advantage. But they have not responded to the unmerited blessings that God has bestowed upon them. They have been full of rebellion, ingratitude, and forgetfulness of God; and still He has dealt with them as a loving, forgiving father deals with an ungrateful, wayward son. They have resisted His grace, abused His privileges, slighted His opportunities, and have been satisfied to sink down in contentment, in lamentable ingratitude, hollow formalism, and hypocritical insincerity."[17]

Indeed, this message is a wake-up call and a sober reminder to an insipid, powerless, self-absorbed people, characterized by an altogether wrong mind-set. Their ecclesiastical pride gives them the false assurance that they are in the driver's seat in the religious world, when, in fact, they are woefully self-deceived, misguided, and desperately in need. Based on the evidence of the True and Faithful Witness, there is an urgent need for mental adjustment among the people of God. The only antidote for this mind-set is to heed the counsel of the True and Witness Himself—that is, to seek out the heavenly merchantman, and buy from Him gold tried in the fire, white raiment, and heavenly eyesalve.[18] Taken together, these represent the total mind and character of Jesus Christ, who says to us all: "Take my yoke upon you and *learn from me*; for I am *gentle* and *humble* in heart, and you will find rest unto your soul" (Matt 11:29, NASB, italics mine).

Richard Rice rightly suggests, "as we seek to understand other religions, we should not approach them with an attitude of smugness or self-congratulation. Our confidence in the truth of Adventism, at best, may offer us a sense of security, but not one of superiority. With the right attitude we can engage in a real dialogue with members of other faiths. We can listen as well as speak."[19] In this matter, we can learn so much from our Master. He who was, and still is, the fountain of all wisdom and knowledge never flaunted His credentials nor postured any form of superiority in the company of friends or foes. He found avenues to His hearers' hearts by treating them with utmost kindness and humble respect.

Our Master's unassuming, disarming approach to an expert Jewish lawyer, who was putting Him to the test was: *"What is written in the Law? How readest thou?"* (Luke 10:26, KJV, italics mine). This approach kept the lawyer's reputation intact and made him feel important enough to open the door of his mind to receive the seed of truth that Jesus was about to sow therein. What a way Christ had with people! He invites us to *learn from Him* (Matthew 11:29). "In My kingdom the principle of preference and supremacy has no place. The only greatness is the greatness of humility. The only distinction is found in devotion to the service of others."[20] "Christ's method alone will give true success in reaching people."[21] Our call is a call to servant leadership.

To ALL People Everywhere

For many decades, Seventh-day Adventist evangelism has been honing in on other Protestant denominations and the Catholic Church, and this may be more by practice than by design. Traditionally, pastors and members of our community of faith have been trained to enunciate and defend the church's doctrinal position, and to call God's people out of Babylon—often viewed as Catholicism, and apostate Protestantism. The evangelistic warpath has been trodden again and again under the uncompromising battle cry: "Come out of her my people!" (Rev 18:4 KJV). Clifford Goldstein says that "the Adventist church does teach . . . that all other denominations are in some degree of theological apostasy, that Adventism alone possesses 'the present truth,' and that through the remnant church, He [God] proclaims a message that is to restore His true worship by calling His people out of the apostasy and preparing them for Christ's return."[22]

This philosophy is much in keeping with the position and image the early church pioneers tried to create in order to clearly establish an identity for the young church of advent believers after the 1844 disappointment. This identity was to be distinct and separate from that of the other denominations of the day, so our pioneers placed a very strong emphasis on defining and enunciating church doctrine. However, though the church has strongly established itself around the world, this posture or positioning strategy has not changed over the years. We still seek to define ourselves in terms of our doctrines and theological differences from other Protestant religions, rather than by our relation to Christ and our ability to reflect His love in our daily contact with humanity. Thus, our evangelism has taken on a more doctrinal, and often confrontational, approach.

Typically, Adventist evangelism presupposes that the targeted individuals or audiences have a Christian background or orientation, or at least believe in the authority of the Bible. These presuppositions become prerequisites, since it would be rather difficult, or nearly impossible, to present the Third Angel's Message without either of these basic frameworks. It is not surprising, therefore, that our evangelistic success has occurred predominantly with Catholics and other Protestants, with very little or no showing from the secular un-Christian world. Because church leaders and members are not generally trained to work with the people from non-Christian religions, the secular-minded, or the unchurched, they tend to ignore them in their evangelistic planning and process. However, the growing presence of these people groups in contemporary societies around the world is no longer an issue that can be easily glossed over, ignored, or wished away. As a matter of fact, ignoring any people group, when it has to do with the *Missio Dei,* is not a valid option for us, since the divine call of the remnant mandates the preaching of the everlasting gospel to every person (Revelation 14:6).

Lift up Your Eyes and See

The ministry of Jesus challenges us to take off the spiritual blinders and engage our thoughts to focus on, and work for, all classes of people, and especially those who appear to be different from us. There is a tendency among many Christians, including Seventh-day Adventists, to focus their evangelistic ministries on individuals whom they perceive can fit into their fellowship circle. They just do not feel comfortable rubbing shoulders with people who are socially and culturally different from themselves.

In a special issue of *View* magazine, titled "Movement—Is There Room for Me in Your Church?"[23] César González wrote a very moving story of a teenage gangster who decided to visit an eXcite98 event, in a desperate attempt to ditch his past gang affiliation and to find a new life for himself. However, as soon as he arrived at this great youth event, he was accosted by a seasoned church member, who heaped on him a barrage of "holy" insults, because of the tattoos that were imprinted on his face, neck, and arms. Fortunately, but very narrowly, the young man survived this unwelcome attack and went on to have an enjoyable experience at the week-long event. However, before he left for home, he had this message for the Seventh-day Adventist Church, through César, his newly found friend: "I would like to tell them [church members] that the Church is for sinners. I would tell them that the worse shape someone is in, the more help they need. I would tell them to be more forgiving and less judgmental. There is no need for that in the Church, that's what cops and judges are for.[24]

How many more incidents like this occur in Christian communities on a regular basis? Christians allow nonessential, non-salvation issues to cloud their view of a sinner's need for Christ and salvation. Bill Hull says, "we have erected unnecessary barriers between ourselves and the very ones we pray to reach. These barriers are usually cultural, not theological. We often communicate a legalistic attitude that says, 'If you practice certain activities, you are not welcome in the Christian community.' Therefore, the non-believer receives an inflexible, judgmental attitude from the very ones who should be accepting him. The Christian community must keep the unbeliever's view of salvation uncluttered with cultural biases."[25]

When Jesus began His ministry among His people, He found them to be perpetrators of a most severe form of people blindness. Jewish prejudice, bigotry, and exclusivism had blinded the chosen people from seeing and relating to the needs of people who were ethnically and socially different from them. All non-Jews were considered heathens and, therefore, were excluded from the favor of divine grace. Jesus gave several lessons to His disciples, often in the presence of the masses, to challenge this mind-set which is still very present in some Adventist circles in the form of racism, and ethnic and cultural indifference.

In His ministry to the Syrophoenician woman (Matt 15:21-28), Christ showed that all barriers must be broken down so that the good news of the gospel could have free and complete access to all peoples of the earth, regardless of race, color, or creed. Ellen White states, "caste is hateful to God. He ignores everything of this character. In His sight, the souls of all men are of equal value."[26] There is absolutely no room for people blindness here. Jesus' actions completely nullify this mind-set. Mrs. White further explains that Jesus' response to the need of the Gentile woman "opened the minds of the disciples more fully to the labor that lay before them among the Gentiles. They saw a wide field of usefulness outside of Judea. They saw souls bearing sorrows unknown to those more highly favored. Among those whom they had been taught to despise were souls longing for help from the mighty Healer, hungering for the light of truth, which had been so abundantly given to the Jews."[27]

The Master launched another major attack on Jewish blind prejudice when He deliberately chose to make a detour through the land of Samaria, on His way to Galilee (see John 4). Although Samaria lies along the path that formed the shortest route from Judea to Galilee, the Jews generally chose other routes to avoid having to encounter the Samaritans. However, Jesus chose this route because He had a definite purpose in mind, and a very important lesson to teach His disciples. His compassion for the lost constrained Him to choose the path of ministry and not the route of prejudicial blindness and avoidance. In His encounter with the woman at Jacob's well, He again illustrated the fact that absolutely no boundaries should inhibit the mission of God and the proclamation of the gospel. Jon Paulien observes, "Right from the start, the woman had three strikes against the possibility that she might develop a relationship with Jesus. She was a woman in a public place, she was a member of a hated race, and she was living in sin. No respectable Jewish man would have been caught speaking to her. But Jesus took the risk of reaching across all these barriers to provide for her the living water that He had come to give to whoever was willing to believe."[28]

Evidently, Jesus allowed none of the cultural, ethnic, or political issues that embroiled His race to cloud His vision, or deter His ministry to a struggling sinner in dire need of rescue and salvation. The account says that through this adulterous woman, Jesus was introduced to an entire Samaritan village. Ellen White comments, "the Samaritan woman proved herself a more effective missionary than His own disciples. The disciples saw nothing in Samaria to indicate that it was an encouraging field. Their thoughts were fixed upon a great work to be done in the future. They did not see that right around them was a harvest to be gathered. But through the woman they despised, a whole cityful was brought to hear the Saviour. She carried the light at once to her countrymen."²⁹ How grossly people-blind these disciples were, and while they stood there, questioningly taking in the closing scene of Jesus' dialogue and the subsequent exodus of Samaritan villagers coming to hear Him, He challenged their Jewish prejudice with the words: "Do you not say, There are yet four months, and then comes the harvest? Behold, I say to you, lift up your eyes, and look on the fields, that they are white for harvest" (John 4: 35 NASB).

These words of Christ were not limited to His disciples only, but they represent a call to every born-again Christian to take off the spiritual, cultural, ethnic, and social blinders, and to lift up our eyes and look unto the fields that are white and ready for harvest. We need to lift up our eyes and see the multitudes of unreached people who are drinking from the broken cistern of this ungodly world, and then we must tax our intellect and resources to find ways and means to reach out to them with the saving gospel of Jesus Christ. Mrs. White makes it clear that "we are called upon to lift our eyes to the 'regions beyond.' Christ tears away the wall of partition, the dividing prejudice of nationality, and teaches a love for all the human family. He lifts men from the narrow circle that their selfishness prescribes; He abolishes all territorial lines and artificial distinctions of society. He makes no difference between neighbors and strangers, friends and enemies. He teaches us to look upon every needy soul as our brother, and the world as our field."³⁰

There is absolutely no excuse for an attitude that is insensitive, blind, or unresponsive to needs of sinners entrapped in the intricacies of the kingdom of darkness. The peoples of non-Christian religions, the secular, the gangster, and the profligate are all souls for whom Christ has died, and for whom heaven will expend its best gifts to save. Any mind-set that overlooks or turns away from these people needs complete realignment with the all-embracing, compassionate mind of Christ. Our mission mandate clearly summons us to be very intentional in developing approaches to reach secular, un-churched people, and in creating loving communities to receive and nurture them.

Enemies or Partners In The Gospel?

In chapter 2, I briefly outlined the evolution of the polemic that our pioneers developed against Roman Catholicism and Protestantism, characterizing both as the "mystical system of Babylon."[31] From that time to this present day, we have sought to maintain a great gulf between that system and us, and have made it the pivotal focus of our evangelistic thrusts.

Although we have a sound theological position with reference to the fall of Babylon, it does not justify the spirit of hostility and religious indifference that has characterized our relations with Catholics and Protestants over the years. We keep ourselves separate and aloof from them, and strain our efforts not to be associated, or be counted as one, with them in any public forum. Church leaders and pastors have also contributed to this spirit of rivalry when promoting and conducting evangelistic campaigns. In the church and under the tent we use phrases and labels that communicate to our members that non-Adventists, regardless of their profession, are on the other side of the religious track and that we are up against them in winning souls for the Kingdom of God. An official statement released at the last General Conference Session held in Toronto, Canada, admonished the church against such unbecoming behavior. The statement read: "Evangelistic and missionary activity needs to respect the dignity of all human beings. Individuals need to be truthful and transparent when dealing with other religious groups. *Terminology* should be used which *avoids offending* other religious communities. Statements which are false or ridicule other religions should not be made"[32] (italics mine).

This spirit has created unnecessary hostility toward Seventh-day Adventists in the past, and church members have mistakenly attributed that hostility to "the dragon that is wrath with the woman and went to make war with the remnant of her seed" (Rev 12:17). However, there is absolutely no Christian virtue to be derived from hostility that is self-induced. Peter tells us: "For this is thankworthy, if a man for conscience toward God endure grief, suffering wrongfully. For what glory is it, if, when ye be buffeted for your faults, ye shall take it patiently? But if, when ye do well, and suffer for it, ye take it patiently, this is acceptable with God" (1 Pet 2:19, 20 KJV). Ellen White counsels us: "Be ye therefore wise as serpents, and harmless as doves. Do not arouse the malignity of the enemy by making denunciatory speeches. Thus you will close doors against the entrance of truth. Clear-cut messages are to be borne. But guard against arousing antagonism. There are many souls to be saved. *Restrain all harsh expressions.* In word and deed be wise unto salvation, *representing Christ to all* with whom you come in contact"[33] (italics mine).

This has been a major issue with our evangelistic strategies in the past and still does persist in some areas of the world. For example, when new converts are won through our evangelistic exploits, we immediately inoculate them from any affiliation with their former Christian associates and friends. Sometimes these converts are used to testify against their former brethren as an evangelistic strategy, with the hope that it would encourage others to join the church. These new converts assume that in order for them to be fully incorporated into the believing Adventist community they need to adopt the "us-against-them" mental framework. This phenomenon encourages them to look at their former religious experience, together with their communal associations, in a very negative light and sets them up to speak very disparagingly of the same.

Therefore, it is not very surprising to find that in our Adventist communities there are hosts of believers who have practically severed all relationships with their former Christian friends and neighbors and have never looked back to initiate any meaningful contact with them—evangelistic or otherwise. As a Christian community, we have unwittingly concentrated more on trying to maintain our denominational uniqueness based on physical separation than on Christ-centered living and effective discipleship. In effect, we have perpetuated an unhealthy mentality that conflicts with our mission.

In His deliverance of the Gerasene demoniacs, Jesus enunciated a very important and powerful mission principle. Immediately following their deliverance, these once possessed men begged Jesus to take them along with Him (probably hoping to learn at His feet and become a part of Jesus' discipleship team), but the Master's response was: *"Go home to your people and report to them what great things the Lord has done for you, and how he had mercy on you."* (Mark 5:19 NASB). Although these two men did not receive any formal instruction or indoctrination, they had a story to tell about the saving power of Jesus, and Jesus *trusted* them enough to tell the story even among their heathen country people.

In describing Christ's commission of these two new converts, Ellen White clearly states, "the two restored demoniacs were the first missionaries whom Christ sent to preach the gospel in the region of Decapolis. For a few moments only these men had been privileged to hear the teachings of Christ. *Not one sermon from His lips had ever fallen upon their ears.* They could not instruct the people as the disciples who had been daily with Christ were able to do. But they bore in their own persons the evidence that Jesus was the Messiah. They could tell what they knew; what they themselves had seen, and heard, and felt of the power of

Christ. This is what everyone can do whose heart has been touched by the grace of God"[35] (italics mine).

Christ's two-fold command to His disciples is not come and *stay* (away), but come and *go* (back)! Indeed "every true disciple is born into the kingdom of God as a missionary. He who drinks of the living water becomes a fountain of life. The receiver becomes a giver. The grace of Christ in the soul is like a spring in the desert, welling up to refresh all, and making those who are ready to perish eager to drink of the water of life."[36] However, when we cut individuals off from the communities from which they were extracted, by replicating the "us-against-them" mind-set, we are not only doing them disservice, but we are cutting off the very means by which those communities can be reached with the living gospel of Jesus Christ.

The woman at Jacob's well and the Gerasene demoniacs all testify to this fact. It is very significant to observe that while Jesus Himself was rejected by the people of Gerasene, they embraced His new disciples (two of their own), whose powerful witness and testimony set the region of Decapolis ablaze with the gospel, and prepared that locality as a fruitful field for their Master's second visit.[37] This episode is particularly instructive for traditional Christians living in a postmodern society, since they have an extremely difficult time trying to reach untraditional, secular people for the kingdom of God. The best people to reach secular people for Christ are secular people who have been saved by Christ. New believers should, therefore, be trained and encouraged to return to the communities from which they were captured by the gospel, to share the good news of their testimony in Jesus Christ. While the idea of isolating new converts from neighbors and friends may be well-intentioned, it is not in keeping with the gospel order practiced by Jesus.

It appears rather confusing to the outside observer that while we readily admit that we are not the only Christians proclaiming Christ to the world (our official theology), we do, by our actions, relate to Protestants and Catholics as though they are not Christians (our unofficial theology). In other words: "We are like you, but not really like you." This confusion is a mere reflection of the identity crisis that is resident in Adventism. We seek an identity that is separate and different from the rest of Christianity, yet we want to be regarded as Christians. There appears to be some confusion with regard to integrating our mission with our true identity. Many of our believers prefer and hold to an identity based on our mission (Adventism, or the Advent message to all the world), rather than one based on our Founder, Jesus Christ. Thus, so many would rather be identified as Adventists rather than Christians—relating to the two positions as mutually exclusive experiences even though they should not be. To admit that I am a Christian is tantamount to admitting that I am just another Protestant believer, and all this in an effort to stress my "Adventistness." By such an admission I have made my Christianity subject to Adventism, instead of the other way around.

The unwelcome truth is that the Christianity of the

Bible is not subject to any of the modern-day "isms" and their cohorts of followers. Rather, all of Christendom, regardless of denomination or profession, must be guided by the principles of Christ, the originator of Christianity. Consequently, there is no other authentic identity for the follower of Christ than the one called Christian. Any other pseudo-identity as espoused by Protestant denominations finds its meaning only in their doctrinal position and not the person of Jesus Christ. The early believers in Antioch followed Christ so closely, and spoke of Him so often that they were given the name Christians (Acts 11:26). That was their identity! The reality of their identity was based upon the indwelling life of their risen Savior that Holy Spirit was reproducing in them.

Must the "remnant" of that early church subscribe to an identity that is any different? Our mission may be somewhat dissimilar to that of the early church and even modern-day Protestantism, but our identity is very much the same—it is still Christian! Our mission, not our identity, is what distinguishes us from other Christian communities, and this needs to be clearly understood by all our people. We share more in common with other Christians than that which sets us apart from them. However, if we are not sure about our identity, we will find ourselves living the "Christian" experience with a denominational "chip" on our shoulders that amplifies our differences because of the unfounded fear of being regarded as "mere" Christians.

In many places around the world, we practice mission

on the basis of our unofficial theology, evidenced in our "us-against-them" mind-set. It may appear rather easy, to the point of gratifying, for us to think that since the "system of Babylon" has fallen, it may be in our best interest to verbally attack and physically separate ourselves from people who are still mesmerized by the wine dispensed from Babylon's mystical fountain. However, Ellen White would remind us, "there are God-fearing men in the fallen churches. If this were not so, we should not be given the message to bear, 'Babylon the great is fallen, is fallen. . . . Come out of her, *My people*.'"[38] The implications of this statement suggest that even though Babylon is fallen, God is still actively at work in that tottering, mystical structure, seeking and saving *His people* (even in Babylon) for *His Kingdom* (not just the "remnant church").

Over and over again, we have been characterized and labeled as possessing a spirit of religious arrogance and bigotry, not so much because of what we believe, but more so because of our separatist, unfriendly, condescending attitude toward Christians from other denominations. They view us with grave suspicion and often form very unhealthy images as to what Seventh-day Adventism is all about, and, on not too few occasions, have labeled us as a cult religion. This negative outlook of the church has created some really difficult situations for effective ministry among people of other faiths and the faithless. It would be rather naive, bordering on arrogant, for us to just sit by and assume a martyr complex, when, indeed, we have created our own unwelcome situation.

A better approach would be to reach our hands across the gulf, and in the spirit of Jesus, be more neighborly to our fellow Christians and at the same time look for opportunities where we can be partners in ministry to the local, national, and even international community. This is not an appeal for ecumenism, but a plea for God's people to form positive relationships with Christians of other faiths, among whom the Spirit of Jehovah is still actively at work preparing God's invisible remnant for the final events of earth's history.

Ellen White was correct when she stated, "the Lord has His representatives in all the churches. These persons have not had the special testing truths for these last days presented to them *under circumstances that brought conviction to heart and mind; therefore they have not, by rejecting light, severed their connection with God.* Many there are who have faithfully walked in the light that has shone upon their pathway. They hunger to know more of the way and works of God."[39] She also counsels, "*our ministers should seek to come near to the ministers of other denominations. Pray for and with these men, for whom Christ is interceding.* A solemn responsibility is theirs. As Christ's messengers, we should manifest a deep, earnest interest in these shepherds of the flock"[40] (italics mine).

On the contrary, we have generally done the opposite to this counsel and have avoided ministerial associations and assemblies, where pastors from various denominations attempt to work together for personal enrichment, ministry enhancement, and the good of the community. We often assume a posture that suggests that we are better prepared and more informed than other ministers, and portray, by our attitude, that there is little benefit, or anything, for us to learn from these associations. Have we become the Pharisees of the new millennia? Are we saying by our attitude: "Lord, I thank you that I am a minister in your remnant church, and I am not like that preacher over yonder?" I sincerely believe (and earnestly plead) that this mind-set, which draws up battle-lines and builds walls that unnecessarily alienate us from the rest of the Christian community, needs to be replaced by the mind of Christ for three valid reasons:

1. It is contrary to the person and spirit of Jesus Christ, and runs against the grain of Scripture.

Even though Jesus knew that "salvation is from the Jews" (John 4:22 NRSV), He did not treat other marginal or religious groups with any indifference or condescension. He rejected this "us-against-them" attitude when His disciples reported their account of attempting to stop someone (a non-disciple by their standard) from casting out demons in the name of Jesus "because he *followeth not us*"[41] (italics mine). In other words, "this man is not a member of our church, so this work must be of the devil." The disciples expected Christ's commendation, but Jesus used the opportunity to show them that the person casting out devils in His name was not an enemy, but a partner in ministry.

On yet another occasion, the disciples of John the Baptist came to him questioning the authority of Jesus to baptize the people who were flocking after Him, when Jesus, Himself, was baptized by John (John 3:22-26). John's answer to His disciples was very much similar to the answer Jesus gave to His disciples. He said, *"no one can receive anything except what has been given from heaven"* (John 3:27). In both of the above examples we can see the budding spirit of religious intolerance, which essentially formed the fuel for the fires of religious persecution throughout the centuries.

Listen to James and John as they prescribe the "Christian" solution for the rejection of Jesus by a Samaritan village: *"Lord, do You want us to command fire to come down from heaven and consume them"* (Luke 9:51-54)? Ellen White[42] says that these men were surprised to see that Jesus was pained by their word, and still more surprised as His rebuke fell upon their ears, *"Ye know not what manner of spirit ye are of. For the Son of man is not come to destroy men's lives, but to save them"* (Luke 9:55-56). Says Mrs. White: "It is not part of Christ's mission to compel men to receive Him. It is Satan, and men actuated by his spirit, that seek to compel the conscience. . . . There can be not more conclusive evidence that we possess the spirit of Satan than the disposition to hurt and destroy those who do not appreciate our work, or who act contrary to our ideas."[43]

2. <u>It is not in the best interest of what Christianity represents for us to set up ourselves as being against the rest of the</u>

Christian community.

One of the strongest arguments that can be forged in favor of Christianity is the genuine unity of Christian believers in a very fragmented and chaotic world. Jesus said: *"By this all men will know that you are My disciples, if you have love one for another"* (John 13:35 NASB). He also said that the unity of believers will serve as a testimony to the world that He came from the Father (see John 17:20-23). However, one of the greatest problems non-Christians and unchurched people have with Christianity is that they have a very hard time dealing with so many denominations that claim to be serving the same God, while, at the same time, trying to tug the non-Christian world in so many different theological directions. These unbelievers view the Christian world as being in chaos, with denominations "knifing" one another as they compete for the souls of non-Christians. When we who claim that we have the truth for these last days (and we do) set ourselves up as being at odds with the rest of the Christian world by our superior, "us-against-them" attitude, we are not making the world's theological mazes any easier for the unsaved who are genuinely seeking after God.

Christ's Kingdom is one, and "a kingdom divided against itself will not stand" (Matthew 12:25). So we cannot project the image that gives any semblance that we are trying to build an Adventist kingdom on earth that rivals the kingdoms of Protestantism and Roman Catholicism. While we do have some distinctive doctrines, which by their very nature, put us at odds with the rest of Christendom, we should endeavor to be more Christlike in the way we relate to people of other faiths.

3. It closes the window of opportunity for enhancing ministry and reaching people of other faiths.

God did not endow only the Seventh-day Adventist Church with all the ideas for effective ministry in these last days. Therefore, if we would accept the challenge of opening up the channel of communication and, to some degree, the opportunity for cooperating with other Christians, there is much that we can learn and teach.

On the other hand, if we persist in an attitude that suggests religious arrogance, it will inhibit our ability to openly listen to and learn from them, and they will be equally unwilling to listen to, or learn from us, regardless of how much truth we believe we have. For example, one of the strong points of our fellow-Christians is their ability to evangelize and to win non-Christians, the secular, and the unchurched. While we do try to reach these groups, with very little success in the West, our primary focus and strength seems to be winning Catholics and Protestants over to Adventism. Is there anything for us to learn here?

Principle of People Priority

One of the most talked about subject in Christian

circles is the love of God for humanity. This love is so deep, so all-embracing and limitless, that it defies human definition, description, and complete comprehension. Yet, as great as God's love is, it cannot exist by itself. It is not selfish by nature and, therefore, needs an object upon which it can express itself. In the beginning, God created because God loved, and still does. Even after the good world He created went bad, God continued to pour out His healing love upon it. John tells us, "God so loved the world that He gave His only Son so that everyone who believes in Him may not perish but have eternal life" (John 3:16 NRSV). *"God proves His love for us in that while we were still sinners Christ died for us"* (Rom 5:8 NRSV).

If there is one fact that we must never lose sight of, it is that God loves the world of sinners and is pouring out heaven's choicest gifts and blessings in order to save them. *People matter to God,*[44] regardless of their station in life. At first glance, this may seem to be a simple truth with which all Christians will agree, but in reality it is a very profound truth that many Christians fail to *own,* far less demonstrate. How many of us, in our daily walk as the followers of Jesus, reflect this truth in the way we relate to people—those who are like us, and, more so, those who are unlike us? Sometimes our attitude reflects the mistaken assumption that God views people (particularly non-Adventists) the way we do, and that He will relate to them as we do. However, we ought to be very mindful of the fact that God is not an Adventist God, nor is He subject to the Adventist world-view. He is much bigger than our field of thought, and our mode of operation.

When God looks down at this world, He does not see people in the human categories of race, color, creed, ethnicity, denomination, political affiliation, or any other line of distinction. Rather He sees all His children—lost children, broken children, hurting children, helpless children, hopeless children and sinful, but redeemed children. He sees a world of people in excruciating pain and will sacrifice anything short of compromising His character to save it. People matter to God, and when we come to *really UNDERSTAND and OWN this truth*, then we will treat people the way Christ did. Moreover, we will consider nothing too dear or too sacred to be freely invested in the cause of saving lost people.

We believe that this God of love has given us a very special end-time message for this judgment-bound world. It is also our belief in this historical position and message that gave birth to the Adventist Church, its mission, and its ministry in the world. For the average Seventh-day Adventist, "the message" (that is, the basic beliefs of the church, with specific emphasis on our distinctive doctrines) is everything, and so much so that quite often the church itself is equated with "the message." For example, one member may ask another: "How long have you been in this message? Or how long have you been in the truth?" ("the message" and "the truth" are treated synonymously in Adventist circles). A member may even try to validate his/her authority as a major decision-maker by making a prefacing statement like: "I have been in 'this message' (or 'the truth') for X number of years . . ." Or when a member apostatizes, it is not quite unusual to hear the statement: "Brother X or Sister Y left 'the message'." What a thing this precious message (or truth) has become!

However, God never intended the gospel, in the context of the Third Angel's Message, to be a glorified end in itself. God is love, and His message to the lost sinners is an extension of that love. The great object of God's love has always been people, and not so much the message He designed to reach them. Like the love of God, the message cannot stand by itself. It can never be an end in itself; it always needs an object to act upon, and without it, the message becomes useless. The object of the Third Angel's Message is the nation, kindred, tongue, and people[45] it is intended to reach. The message exists only because sinners, who need to be saved, exist. If we lose sight of the object of the message, we will become like another people who held in their hands the lifeless forms and traditions of their forefathers, without any power or influence to effect positive changes on their generation.

Interestingly, Vinoth Ramachandra makes this very insightful comment: "The legitimate fear that many have of any claim to absolute truth derives from the historical observation that such claims have led to intellectual tyranny and social repression. But enough has been said to indicate that the logic of the gospel leads us in a different direction. We have seen how the claim of Jesus to absolute truth and, therefore, an absolute authority, was expressed in the form of lowly, sacrificial service. The community that has been brought into being by this truth and entrusted with it for the sake of others can only proclaim that truth in the way of Jesus. Truth is not only embodied in a community, but in a community that relinquishes power in identification with the powerless."[46]

We stand in very critical danger of repeating the sad history of the Jewish nation. There is a tendency for many in our fellowship to equate Adventism and "the truth" to our remnancy in much the same manner as the Jews equated Judaism and its laws to their temple. The Jews trusted in the security of their temple and rejected the One for whom it was built and to whom it pointed. We are in critical danger of placing more confidence in the certainty of the Third Angel's Message than we do in Christ as our Substitute and Sufficiency. Just as the Jews wanted the world to be attracted to Jerusalem because of the beauty and grandeur of their temple, we stand in grave danger of wanting the world to be attracted to Adventism by the beauty and power of our message. The Jews blew their mission by hiding behind the complex of their temple. We face the impending danger of blowing our mission by hiding behind the complex of our message.

The Jews mission was completely Judeo-centric because it was centered on the heritage, history and traditions which defined them instead upon the eternal purpose of the One Who gave birth to the nation, and Who was the only reason for its existence. Thus, Israel's leaders and people spent their lives propagating, protecting, and preserving Judaism instead of blessing the world with the knowledge of God. Sadly, we are not in a better position today than Israel was prior to, and during, the time of Christ. We too have chosen to define ourselves more by our historical heritage and traditions instead of by the One who birthed Christianity. We too spend our years propagating and defending the system of Adventism and the uniqueness of the Remnant Church, instead of proclaiming the power and grace of the saving Christ, and of seeking to build His Kingdom—not ours. As a result, the simple message of the gospel often becomes so cluttered and encumbered by our pre-occupation with our denominational distinctiveness, that our hearers fail to see the saving Christ in the message we proclaim.

God's message to Israel, in the days of Jeremiah, is so pertinent for us today:

> Amend your ways and your deeds, and I will let you dwell in this place [the temple]. Do not trust in deceptive words, saying, "This is the temple of the Lord, the temple of the Lord, the temple of the Lord [and it was indeed]." For if you truly amend your ways and your deeds, if you truly practice justice between a man and his neighbor. If you do not oppress the alien, the orphan, or the widow, and do not shed innocent blood in this place [the temple], nor walk after other gods to your own ruin, then I will let you dwell in this place, in the land that I gave to

your fathers forever and ever.

Behold you are trusting in deceptive words to no avail. Will you steal, murder, and commit adultery, and swear falsely, and offer sacrifices to Baal, and walk after other gods that you have not known, then come and stand before Me in this house, which is called by My name, and say, "We are delivered!"—that you may do all these abominations?

Has this house, which is called by My name, become a den of robbers in your sight? Behold, I even I, have seen it, declares the Lord. (Jeremiah 7:3-11 NASB)

It was God's original design that the Jewish temple (the house that was called by His name) would be a gathering place for worship and prayer for all people, including the foreigner who did not belong to Israel.[47] The temple was to be called "An house of prayer for *ALL PEOPLE*" (Isaiah 56:7). The value of the house was linked to its faithful representation of the One for whom it was built, and to whom it pointed. However, the leaders of Israel used the "name" of the house as a cover for injustice, abuse, oppression, idolatry, and all kinds of wickedness. The name of the house was used in a way to give the worshipers a false sense of security in the face of apostasy. Thus, instead of being a house of prayer for all people, the temple became a shallow symbol of Jewish pride and self-deception. The multitudes that came to the temple year after year to seek after God went away empty, with unrealized hopes.

However, Malachi prophesied that *"the Lord, whom ye seek, shall suddenly come to His temple, even the Messenger of the covenant, whom ye delight in: behold, He shall come, saith the Lord of hosts. But who may abide the day of His coming? And who shall stand when He appeareth? For He is like a refiner's fire, and like fullers' soap: and He shall sit as a refiner and purifier of silver: and He shall purify the sons of Levi, and purge them as gold and silver"* (Malachi 3:1-3).

In direct fulfillment of this prophecy, Jesus paid a surprise visit to His temple and caught the Jewish leaders and temple officials in the midst of their sin and corruption. With divine authority, He drove out the extortioners, leaders, and temple officials, echoing the very words of Isaiah: *"It is written, My house shall be called a house of prayer; but you are making it a robbers' den"* (Matt. 21:13 NASB). As the "Messenger of the covenant," Jesus came to purge His temple and restore its order. What a change Christ's presence had wrought! The priests and their cohorts had fled the scene and Jesus alone stood as the center of His temple. The poor and the disenfranchised that remained behind then flocked to Jesus, the true Shepherd of the sheep, and had all their needs met. The love of God was dispensed freely and without partiality, as healing grace flowed from Christ upon the hungry, waiting multitude.

What is God's message to His remnant people today?

The True and Faithful Witness says we are woefully self-deceived regarding our true condition.[48] God's message to us at this time, most logically, might say: "Do not trust in deceptive words, saying we are the remnant people of God, we have the message, we have the truth [and indeed we do, just as the Jews had the temple], we have need of nothing! Amend your ways of self-congratulation, self-sufficiency, and self-righteousness. Behold you are trusting in deceptive words to no avail. Will you practice racism, boastful pride, materialism and sensuality, and engage in all forms of injustice and inequity? And then stand in this place and say: 'We are the remnant, we have the truth,' while you stand guilty before Me in all these things? Amend your ways and your doings, lest I spew you out of my mouth!"

    I humbly appeal to the members of my church family to let Christ, His righteousness and His glory be the dominant center and theme of our *message*, of our *mind-set*, and of *our mission practice*. Christ must be all in all. He must be the living reality reflected in the lives we live, in the message we proclaim, and in our approach to reaching and ministering to people. Mrs. White puts it this way: "The sacrifice of Christ as an atonement for sin is the great truth around which all other truths cluster. In order to be rightly understood and appreciated, every truth in the Word of God, from Genesis to Revelation, must be studied in the light that streams from the cross of Calvary. I present before you the great, grand monument of mercy and regeneration, salvation and redemption—the Son of God uplifted on the cross. This is to

be the foundation of every discourse given by our ministers
. . . Christ and His righteousness—*let this be our platform, the very life of our faith*"⁵⁰ (emphasis mine).

She further stated that the Third Angel's Message was "to bring more prominently before the world the uplifted Saviour, the sacrifice for the sins of the whole world. It presented justification through faith in the Surety; it invited the people to receive the righteousness of Christ, which is made manifest in obedience to all the commandments of God. *Many had lost sight of Jesus.* They needed to have their eyes directed to His divine person, His merits, and His changeless love"⁵¹ (emphasis mine). Never should we stray away from these timeless counsels. To do so will shipwreck of our faith—a sad repetition of Jewish history.

We must be constantly reminded that the message, which many among us refer to as the truth, is embodied in the person of Jesus Christ. Truth is not just something we believe. Rather, it is embodied in the life we live. Christ was the Father's message, the Father's truth. He was and is the Only Truth that there is, and He never placed Himself above the people of His day. In fact, Jesus was the truth that came down from heaven, took on the garb of humanity, and became one with the human family. In Jesus, truth condescends (John 1:14), truth ministers and serves (Matt 20:28), truth rebukes (Matt 23; John 8: 44-47), truth forgives (Mark 2:1-11; John 8:1-11), truth uplifts (Mark 14:3-9), truth teaches (Matt 5-7), and truth saves (Matt 18:11; Luke 23:42, 43). Christ's ministry did not attract the masses simply because He spoke the truth with clarity and power, but mainly because He lived the truth. Truth was never exalted above the people, but was always in the service of uplifting and building them. Charles E. Bradford says, "there can be no doubt about our theological framework. We have the truth. Proclamation is important. But the end result must be a people who have learned to live together in Christian love."[52]

At the end of the day, what will really count with God is not the message and how we know or proclaim it, but rather the people who have been saved and transformed by believing and living it. This is the greatest evidence, the proof positive, the most incontrovertible argument that can be advanced in favor of the gospel. When a Christian community which espouses the truth can live the truth in love as Jesus did, then that community bears the undisputable witness that it truly the remnant, the last remaining disciples of Jesus Christ (Revelation 12:17; John 13:35).

Notes

1. Barna, *Marketing the Church*, 27.
2. Kotler and Levy, 15.
3. The does not intend to make a wholesale application of all the principles of marketing management to the life and work of the body of Christ, for such an application may violate the high sense of moral integrity and spiritual fervor that accompanies the sacred task of proclaiming the gospel and incorporating believing men and women into the Kingdom of God. The study will attempt to examine and transfer key marketing principles, concepts and strategies to the marketing of services, persons and ideas in a

religious context. This will involve a refining of meaning and application of commonly used marketing terms so that they can find relevance and acceptance in a religious setting. Thus, marketing will be used only as a tool for maximizing the utility of the available resources of the witnessing Christian community for fulfilling the *Missio Dei.*

4. Barna, 13-14.
5. Mission from *outside in* will be treated with greater detail in the next chapter.
6. Bill Hybels, *Honest to God? Becoming an Authentic Christian* (Grand Rapids: Zondervan, 1990), 125.
7. See Goldstein, 168.
8. Millard J. Erickson, *Does It Matter If God Exists?* (Grand Rapids: Baker Books, 1996), 34.
9. It is important to note that these disciples received the baptism of John, nut not the baptism of Jesus Christ, in His name, nor in the name of the Holy Spirit. The complete baptismal formula (Matthew 28:19, 20) instituted by Jesus Christ did not characterize the experience of John's disciples. These conscientious followers of John were not even aware of the existence of the Holy Spirit and He was a very significant exclusion as the only guarantor of their religious experience (Ephesians 1:13, 14).
10. White, *Desire of Ages,* 62-63.
11. Ibid., 63.
12. Ibid., 819-820.
13. White, *Testimony to the Church* 9:190.
14. Christopher J. H. Wright, "The Christian and Other Religions: the Biblical Evidence," *Themelios* 9:2 (1984), 7.
15. See Revelation 3:14-22.
16. See Uriah Smith, "The Last Way-Marks," *Review and Herald,* December 11, 1856, 44; and Waggoner to Smith, *Review and Herald,* December 25, 1856, 61.
17. Ellen White, *Selected Messages,* vol. 1 (Washington, DC: Review and Herald Publishing Association, 1958), 357.
18. Ibid., 358.
19. Richard Rice, *The Reign of God* (Berrien Springs, MI: Andrews University Press, 1997), 215.
20. White, Desire of Ages, 650.
21. Ellen White, *The Ministry of Healing* (Mountain View, CA: Pacific Press Publishing Association, 1942), 143.
22. Clifford Goldstein, *The Remnant* (Bise, ID: Pacific Press Publishing Association, 1994), 12.
23. Céasar González, "A Sinner Among Saints, " *View* (Silver Spring, MD: North American Division of Seventh-day Adventists, 1999),

12-15, 22.
24. Ibid.
25. Bill Hull, *Jesus Christ, Disciplemaker* (Grand Rapids: Fleming H. Revell, 1990), 101.
26. White, *Desire of Ages*, 403.
27. Ibid., 402.
28. Jon Paulien, *The Abundant Life Bible Amplifier–John* (Boise, ID: Pacific Press Publishing Association, 1995), 103.
29. White, *Desire of Ages*, 195.
30. Ibid., 823.
31. Revelation 17:3-6. See also pp. 27-28.
32. Part of the official statement on Religious Liberty, Evangelism, and Proselytism voted by the General Conference of Seventh-day Adventists Administrative Committee (ADCOM), for release at the time of the General Conference Session in Toronto, Canada, June 29-July 9, 2000.
33. White, *Manuscript* 6, 1902.
34. See Matthew 8:28-34 and Mark 5:1-20 for the entire account of the incident.
35. White, *Desire of Ages*, 340.
36. Ibid., 195.
37. Ibid., 297.
38. White, *Evangelism*, 559.
39. White, *Testimony to the Church* 6:70-71.
40. Ibid., 78.
41. See Mark 9:38-42.
42. White, *Desire of Ages*, 487.
43. Ibid.
44. See Mark Mittelberg's expansion of this evangelistic value in his book *Building A Contagious Church: Revolutionizing the Way we View and Do Evangelism*, (Grand Rapids: Zondervan Publishing House, 2000), 35-37.
45. See Revelation 14:6-12.
46. Ramachandra, 275.
47. See Isaiah 56:1-8.
48. We have always associated the message to Laodicea (See Revelation 3:14-22) with the remnant church. Laodicea represents the church that does not know that does not know.
49. See John 14:6. Jesus uses the Gr. '*Ego Eimi*,' projecting the idea that He is what the truth is, and apart from Him there is no truth.
50. White, *Evangelism*, 190
51. Ibid.
52. Charles E. Bradford, "Religion in a Secular Age," *Adventist Review*, August 30, 1990, 18.

5

SHIFTING OUR MISSION PARADIGM

The traditional Adventist mission paradigm takes its departure from the church's self-understanding of being God's remnant people with a mandate to proclaim a special end-time message to the whole world. However, the approach to this mission enterprise has been largely message-centered, with an orientation toward the church as an organization. The intent of this chapter is to encourage church administrators, pastors, and lay-people to pursue a mission paradigm that is more people-centered and not allow the demands of traditionalism, formalism, or denominationalism to inhibit us from ministering to the needs of lost humanity.

Tim Wright explains, "tradition keeps the church rooted while it seeks to do ministry in the present. In some congregations however, tradition becomes equated with gospel. Where the institution-driven congregation focuses on maintaining the institution, the tradition-driven church sees its mission as preserving tradition for tradition sake. Rather than translating these traditions into new forms for new generations, these congregations fight to keep the traditions as they have always been. Tradition becomes an anchor, holding the church to the past, rather than a rudder guiding it into the future."¹

There are great days ahead for the Seventh-day Adventist Church around the world; but we must be willing to take an honest, critical look at the traditional ways of doing mission and ministry, and ask all the difficult, but relevant, questions regarding our presence, purpose, and realistic mission accomplishments. For example:

(1) Why do we exist as a church in a particular community?

(2) What is our purpose, and are we accomplishing it to the best of our ability?

(3) Why is it that typical attendance at our church services is so scant?

(4) Why is it that our young people seem to be losing interest in the traditional church services and Adventist Youth meetings (where they exist)?

(5) Why are so many of our members leaving the church? What are the real reasons for their departure?

(6) Why do we continue to spend a large budget on evangelistic tent crusades and baptize mainly a certain class of people?

(7) Why are we finding it so difficult to attract the upper classes, the unchurched, or non-Christians to our fellowship?

(8) Why is the church having such a small impact on the Caucasian population of North America and certain parts of Europe?

The list can go on and on, but the point here is

clear, and there is really not any need for me to extend it. Martin Seeley plainly states, "Asking the difficult 'Why?' questions about purpose, meaning, and values—questions about what we believe about ourselves—is seen as crucial as organizations seek to adjust and develop in a time of rapid social and economic change, without losing their essential identity and direction."[2]

However, we must ask these questions, for the other alternative is not only detrimental to our existence as a Christian community, but also dangerous to our position as God's appointed agency for His final message of warning to the world. The other alternative is what I choose to call the "ostrich" syndrome—that of burying our heads in our traditional forms and customs, pretending that our people and the world in which they live are not experiencing change.

Wade Clark Roof indicates, "the United States and other Western nations are undergoing massive social and cultural changes. The emergence of a global world, an influx of new immigrants and cultures, widespread changes in values and beliefs, the immense role of the media and visual imagery in shaping contemporary life, and expanding consumer-oriented culture targeting the self as an arena for marketing, the erosion of many traditional forms of community–all point to major realignments in religion and culture."[3] In agreement with this, renowned sociologist, Martin Marty, suggests, "there has been a major shift in the center of religious energy from the communal, the public, and the derivative to the personal, private, and autonomous.

So much so that even while the inherited forms of religion persist and still influence people, the individual seeker and chooser have become increasingly to be in control."[4]

Richard N. Ostling projects the idea that "another future trend is the large and growing minority of younger Americans who define themselves as 'spiritual' but not 'religious,' signaling a quest that is neither limited by nor nurtured by the traditional organized religions of the past. More than any previous generation, Americans age 18 and under are thoroughly detached from traditional Christian concepts. By and large they do not believe Jesus is the unique savior of mankind, do not read the Bible as God's word, and do not accept the idea of moral absolutes. Whether one views that as progress or regress depends on one's own concepts of Christianity, reality, and the cosmos. But it is certainly another revolution in our time."[5]

Do we dare pretend that the church is not experiencing and encountering change? There is a certain degree of confidence, in my opinion, that is not worth having, and that is the type of confidence that breathes comfort and complacency when there is an imminent need for urgent action in the face of threatening danger. Because of overconfidence and pride in our historical and theological position as a denomination, it has become quite easy for us to ignore the staggering changes in the society about us, and for us to keep a straight course as the mighty Titanic of modern times. We must be willing to admit that not all change is bad. Change may disturb our comfort level, but we must not allow this discomfort to deprive us from reaping the benefits and blessings that creative, well-thought-out change may bring.

When Jesus came to the Jewish nation, it was a time for change,[6] but He was resisted at every turn, by the religious elite and Jewish leadership, who would rather execute Him than change. In one of His addresses to these religious leaders, Jesus said: *"No one sews a patch of unshrunk cloth on an old garment; otherwise the patch pulls away from it, the new from the old, and a worse tear results. And no one puts new wine into old wineskins; otherwise the wine will burst the skins, and the wine is lost, and the skins as well; but one puts new wine into fresh wine skins"* (Mark 2:21-22 NASB).

Through this illustration, Christ was addressing the inflexible, self-righteous, and arrogant mind-set of the Jewish leaders, who stubbornly clung to their traditional forms and customs even though these traditions were losing their hold on the people.[7] Commenting on this episode in Jesus' ministry, Ellen White explains, "the teaching of Christ, though it was represented by the new wine, was not a new doctrine, but the revelation of that which had been taught from the beginning. But to the Pharisees the truth of God had lost its original significance and beauty. To them Christ's teaching was new in almost every respect, and it was unrecognized and unacknowledged. . . . *Until emptied of the old traditions, customs, and practices, they had no place in mind or heart for the teachings of Christ. They clung to the dead forms, and turned away from the living truth and the power of God*"⁸ (italics mine).

Unlike Israel, we should not allow ourselves to become prisoners of the past, stubbornly clinging to forms and traditions without taking the time to evaluate them in light of changing societal needs, wants, and values. We need to adopt a new mind-set that keeps in step with the times while staying faithful to Scripture. We need to find new ways to express old truths so that we can adequately address the concerns of unsaved people. Bill Hull states, "if we want people to hear, we must bring the message to life by restating the truth with great passion and in a language they understand."⁹

This was the essence of Jesus' message to the Scribes and Pharisees: He was repackaging old truths in a new setting that required a new mind-set for assimilation and implementation. As an expert teacher He was very much in tune with the culture, customs, and spirit of His day, and He allowed these factors to inform and influence the way He packaged divine truths to appeal to the needs of His hearers. Scripture testifies, *"the large crowd was listening to him with delight"* (Mark 12:37, NRSV). *"Never has anyone spoken like this!"* (John 7:46, NRSV) was the report given to the chief priests and Pharisees by the temple police who were sent to arrest Jesus, but could not. Jesus' electrifying witness to the gospel that drew away the temple crowds from their hapless Jewish leaders had brought conviction to these would-be captors' hearts.

No doubt, Jesus was a crowd-puller, not only because

God was with Him, but also because He was able to free the gospel from the shackles of Jewish tradition and tailor it to speak to the hungers of the human heart. Like arrows in the hands of a mighty sharp-shooter, the convicting, converting power of the gospel found its target every time.

New Wine in New Wineskins

Now is a time of great opportunity for the Seventh-day Adventist Church to bring hope to a confused, dying world; but now is also a time for creative, but relevant, change. George Barna states, "Clearly, the Christian body cannot hope to have much of an impact if we respond in the same ways we have in the past. These are new challenges, demanding creative, unique responses. The solutions that worked ten or even five years ago will fail in the coming decade."[10] It is a time for us to put new wine in new wineskins, a time to "put new life in old methods."[11] The new wine imagery is a challenge to the church to be more intentional in seeking for alternative methods and approaches for carrying out its mission and ministry, so that the church's programs and services will resonate positively with the needs of a post-modern world. Jesus clearly points out to us that it does not make any good sense to put new wine in old wineskins, since such an action will only waste the wine and do damage to the wineskins (See Mark 2:21-22, NASB).

It would be rather difficult and almost impossible for the church to adopt new methods and approaches to mission and ministry while maintaining the Adventist mind-set characterized by denominational supremacy, "us-against-them" mentality, people-blindness, and the primacy of the message above people. Such an attempt will be met with strong resistance in many areas of the world church. Ellen White counsels that "there are some minds which do not grow with the work but allow the work to grow far beyond them. . . . Those who do not discern and adapt themselves to the increasing demands of the work, should not stand blocking the wheels, and thus hindering the advancement of others."[12]

The teaching of Jesus that admonishes His disciples to put new wine (alternative methods/approaches to the gospel witness) in new wineskins is very pertinent to the church's current mission situation as it exists in a world engulfed in rapid mega-change. These new wineskins represent a call for a shift in the traditional Adventist mental framework to a new mind-set that will be flexible enough to deal with the mission and ministry challenges precipitated by a very complex and swiftly changing world environment.

In a very real sense, though, this new mind-set is not really new. It is simply a call to re-adopt and re-embrace the mind of Christ ("Let this mind be in you which also was in Christ Jesus" Philippians 2:5), which runs against the grain of the parameters that characterize our mind-set. Unlike our typical mind-set, the mind of Christ gives preeminence to all people regardless of color, race, creed, ethnicity, or people-group. It is not arrogant, self-opinionated, antagonistic, lofty, or cliquish; but humble, peaceable, compassionate, and all-embracing.

In His efforts to seek and save the lost, Christ was not influenced by the cultural norms, traditions, or rabbinical teachings of His day. As a free and radical thinker, He broke out of the box of Jewish traditionalism. He even dared to give all, and risk all, for the salvation of lost men and women. Robert G. Lee states, "He [Christ] came to seek and to save that which was lost. The salvation of sinners was more to Him than the glory He had with God before the world was, for He emptied himself of it all; more to Him than the joys of heaven, for He left them all; more to Him than life, for he said: 'I lay down my life;' more to Him than the shining of the Father's countenance, for He willingly leaped into the awful abyss of the wrath and gloom from the depths of which He cried: 'My God! My God! Why hast Thou forsaken me?' Let this mind be in you which was also in Christ Jesus."[13]

Commenting on the mind of Christ as it relates to meeting mission objectives, Ellen White had this to say: "If we humble ourselves before God, and be kind and courteous and tenderhearted and pitiful, there would be one hundred conversions to the truth where now there is only one. But, though professing to be converted, we carry around with us a bundle of self that we regard as altogether too precious to be given up. It is our privilege to lay this burden at the feet of Christ and, in its place, take the character and similitude of Christ. The Savior is waiting for us to do this."[14] This statement is so practically true, so often repeated, and so seldom implemented in our evangelistic outreach efforts to reach non-members.

Sometimes we allow our denominational pride to get in the way of Christian courtesy and Christlike witness—especially when we encounter people of other faith. Often, instead of building bridges to the truth as it is in Christ, we erect walls of separation between believers. However, now is the time—for it is very late—for us to lay aside the burden of denominational pride associated with our mind-set. It is high time for us to take up the challenges and rewards associated with bearing to the world the mind and character of Christ in our mission and ministry endeavors. In addressing the delegates and members of the World Church at the 2000 General Conference session in Toronto, Canada, out-going Secretary G. Ralph Thompson made very strong reference to the fact that this is no time for timid leadership or play-it-safe techniques. We need bold, adventurous leadership that does not shy away from untried methods, for we are people with a deadline and with a hope to share.[15]

Like our Master Teacher, we must be courageous enough to risk thinking outside the box of traditional Adventism. This new way of thinking will stimulate new visioning for mission and ministry. It will also generate fresh, creative mission strategies that will arrest the attention of secular, post-modern people, whose minds and hearts have become "overcharged with surfeiting, and drunkenness, and the cares of this life" (Luke 21:34, KJV). Traditionalism may offer the benefit of contributing to the spiritual mooring of a religious organization, but it also has the tendency to stem the flow of creative energy that is so crucial for organizational survival in a very competitive, changing environment. This is a new and very difficult age, with very strange, intricate issues and philosophies that are captivating the minds of the masses and challenging the mission offensive of the church. It is an age that is characterized by what is presently known as the post-modern condition, which, according to Darill L. Guder and others, includes such dimensions as: "urbanized life with its complex patterns of social relationships, multiple tasks and responsibilities that fragment time and space; an economy shaped and driven by technology and its advances; job, career, and identity defined by professionalized roles and skills; submerged racial and ethnic identities in a stew-pot society; the pervasive influence of change and rapid obsolescence; bureaucratic organizations run by rules and policies; individualized moral values concerning such matters as divorce and sexuality; hunger for some overarching story to give meaning and structure to life."[16]

In this present context, we cannot allow tame, lifeless, perfunctory, and pre-packaged programs or presentations to be the order of the day, but must constantly tax every resource at our disposal to find a variety of ways to engage and hold the attention of this over-stimulated, heedless generation. This rapidly changing, post-modern environment is swiftly and effectively eroding and displacing the positive effects of the traditional forms of religion. As a result, the church must constantly evaluate the forms and customs it employs to communicate the gospel, in order to be clearly understood by a confused and corrupt world. In many cases, we fail to connect with society because we communicate our message on unknown frequencies. The good news of the gospel becomes garbled by the forms, idioms and clichés that are at home in the Adventist world, but very much foreign and unintelligible to our post-modern, secular society. How true are Bonhoeffer's words, "The rusty swords of the old world are powerless to combat the evils of today and tomorrow."[17]

Seventh-day Adventists have a unique communal vocabulary that can only be clearly understood by insiders. When we employ our unique Adventist terminologies and phrases in the communication of the gospel, we often confuse outsiders—whether they are other Christians, secular, or unchurched people. Traditionally, Christians (including Adventists) hold to the idea that the only really inspired Biblical text is the King James Version. They revere its archaic forms of expression as the only legitimate vehicle to communicate the gospel, even though these Victorian forms of expression hardly make any sense to this present generation and have discouraged many a seeker from reading the Bible.

While we do not subscribe to altering the core beliefs and values of Adventism, we must, at the same time, engage in critical contextualization in order to facilitate mission and ministry that are relevant to the needs of the believing community and the un-Christian world. Truth is unchanging, but its presentation may vary according to the historical, social, and cultural context of the intended audience. Donald Miller suggests, "if Christianity is going to survive [this post-modern era of rapid mega change], it must continually reinvent itself, adapting its message to the members of each generation, along with their culture and the geographical setting."[18]

There are some among us who mistakenly view truth (in this case, our message) and traditional forms (our methods of dissemination) as being the same. Any attempt to make traditional forms of expression more relevant to current societal conditions can be tantamount to a call to holy war. These well-intentioned individuals would rather get rid of the change agents, leave, or even die, than change the order of things in the church. This is such a volatile issue for most traditional churches that some mission and church growth specialists sincerely believe that any attempt at church renewal is an exercise in futility. The major stumbling block is the constant tension (and sometimes acute struggle) between the new and the old.[19]

After investing a quarter century in church renewal, Ralph Neighbor came to the very disturbing conclusion that "we must actively abandon the hope that the stagnant Churches can be renewed by painful restructuring and the tacking on of a cell group . . . According to Jesus, it's not possible to put new wine in old wineskins! The plan for the stagnant Church must begin with the wineskin, not the wine. A church cannot effectively mix traditional patterns of Church life with cell group patterns. There must be a deliberate transition . . . The only hope for old wineskins is to pour out the wine they contain into new ones and throw the leaky things away."[20]

Management guru Peter Drucker once said, "some of the toughest problems we face are those created by successes of the past."[21] This may be particularly true of our evangelistic outreach strategy. Tent crusades, or some variation of the same, have traditionally been our prevailing method for evangelizing non-members. While this approach has yielded large harvests of souls in the past, it has not experienced the same measure of success among secular people and the unchurched. Moreover, the law of diminishing marginal returns is evident in present membership gains due to changes in religious consciousness and expression in our current society. People have grown wary of this dominant, confrontational approach and are less inclined to be influenced positively by it. George G. Hunter III observed, "earlier in this century, the Sunday evening evangelistic service, the Sunday school, the revival, the camp meeting, the crusade and one-to-one confrontational evangelism still fit American culture and still gathered souls. Today those traditional approaches to propagating the gospel are all spent forces, or nearly so. Some churches still rely on those approaches, with declining yields; other churches have abandoned those approaches without replacing them."[22]

There was a time when the Swiss watchmakers dominated the world of watch-making for more than sixty years. They made the best watches, led the world in discovering better ways to manufacture gears, bearings, and mainsprings of watches. They were even pioneers in the waterproofing technique and self-winding model watches. By 1968, the Swiss made 65 percent of all watches sold in the world and laid claim to as much as 90 percent of the profits. By 1980, however, the Swiss had laid off thousands of watchmakers and controlled less than 10 percent of the world market. Their profit domination fell to less than 20 percent. Between 1979 and 1981, more than fifty thousand of the sixty-two thousand Swiss watchmakers had lost their jobs. What was responsible for this drastic turn of events? The Swiss had refused to give critical consideration to a new development—the Quartz movement—ironically invented by a Swiss. Because it had no spring and nob, it was rejected because it was too much of a paradigm shift for them to embrace. Seiko, on the other hand, accepted it and, along with a few other companies, became the leader in the watch industry.

The lesson of the Swiss watchmakers is so profound. A past that was so secure, so profitable, so dominant was destroyed by an unwillingness to consider the future. It was more than not being able to make predictions—it was an inability to rethink how they did business. Past success had blinded them to the importance of seeing the implications of the changing world and to admit that past accomplishment was no guarantee of future success.[23]

As with so many other institutions, the biggest dilemma facing the church is the past success of the church,[24] and our community of faith is not immune to this phenomenon. Commenting on this dilemma created by past successes, Bill Hull states, "these words are carried out daily in stalled-out and dying churches. Form leads function along the road to irrelevancy as Satan hands out the directions. In order to remain within their comfort zone, entrenched leaders hang on to old, non-working forms. Many are still hoping that what worked yesterday will work today. Church people sanctify and calcify ministry forms into articles of faith. Any move to change them becomes a holy "call to arms."[25]

Outside In, Upside Down Mission

As we consider shifting our mission paradigm, the suggestion given by Douglas Webster appears rather instructive: "Marketing provides the necessary paradigm shift for moving away from worn-out forms of the traditional church to the seeker-sensitive, exciting church of the 1990s. One reason church marketing may be gaining greater acceptance is that it appears to be the only alternative to a church stuck in the past, resistant to change and ineffective in proclaiming and living the gospel."[26] This paradigm shift involves a moving away from organization or message-centeredness to people-centeredness. This does not mean that we reduce the importance of the church or the message it proclaims, but it does suggest putting them in their appropriate positions. The church and the message it proclaims exist because there is a lost world to be saved for the Kingdom of God. The world does not exist to serve the church, but the church the world.

Thus, the approach to mission should be from the *outside in* and not from the *inside out*. What this means is that mission does not begin because we have a unique message to proclaim, but because there are lost people in need of salvation. Rightly focused, mission always begins with the needs of lost sinners and not with the needs of the church or organization.

There are occasions when churches and pastors conduct crusades in order to reach arbitrary goals set by the Conferences. Quite often, in the process, they baptize individuals, including children, without giving due consideration to their needs or social condition. These people are drawn into a church environment that seldom conducts any real or meaningful appraisal of their needs and is, therefore, unprepared to adequately minister to them. Many of them linger long enough to see what the church is all about, and then they leave. When they do leave, the general tendency is to ascribe their leaving to their lack of understanding of the "message." There is absolutely no consideration given to the fact that the personal and collective ambition of the pastor and the church to satisfy organizational needs overshadowed the needs of the struggling sinner. *This is organization-centered mission, mission from the inside out.*

Sometimes this approach to mission encourages us to go after people who, we think, would benefit us most when they accept the message. Ellen White warns, "the gospel invitation is not to be narrowed down, and presented to a select few, who, we suppose, will do us some honor if they accept it. The message is to be given to all. Wherever hearts are open to receive the truth, Christ is ready to instruct them."[27]

However, *mission from the outside in* focuses more on what is going on with the targeted population and what God is calling the church to do for them. As a matter of fact, this is where all true mission begins—from the outside. Mission did not begin with some divine administrative agenda, but rather with human lostness and desperate need of salvation. A loving God who was willing to risk anything and everything to save us stepped outside of Himself and into our fallen world, in order to redeem His creation.

The Biblical model of the plan of salvation is portrayed in a need-satisfaction framework. The gospel always begins from the point of people's desperate need and God's gracious desire to meet and satisfy it. As a young Christian, one of the very first ways I learned to present the gospel to the unsaved was by a simple acronym called "the ABC of Salvation". Allow me to illustrate:

> **A** - "**A**ll have sinned and fallen short of the glory of God"
> (Rom 3:23 NASB); and "the wages of sin is death" (Rom 6:23 NASB).
> **B** - "**B**ehold the Lamb of God who takes away the sin of the world" (John 1:29 NASB).
> **C** - "**C**ome unto me all who are weary and heavy-laden and I will give you rest" (Matt 11:28 NASB).

The initial focus of this acronym is on the human condition, which is completely need-centered; then on God's provision of the need-satisfier (Jesus the crucified Lamb); and finally the call for a response. It is very important to note that the call for response from the sinner never precedes the sinner's need recognition, or the satisfaction of his need. It is only when person recognizes his utter sinfulness and helplessness (sense of need), and is drawn by the power of God's provision on the cross (satisfaction), that he can intelligently respond to the love that will not let him go. Dan Day has rightly said, "God's message to us is a need-satisfying message. To the degree that we don't couch it in those terms when we communicate it to others, we're confusing people and doing the Lord a disservice"[28]

Although Jesus had a very clear purpose to rescue perishing souls, His ministry to them consistently took its departure from the point of their obvious need. With the woman at the well, He began with water (the thing she desired), but went on to offer her salvation (John 4). With the man born blind, Jesus healed him and later challenged him with the claims of the gospel (John 9). Jesus followed the same pattern with the man at the pool of Bethesda (John 5). Jesus also fed the hungry multitude before ministering the Word to them (John 6).

Although Jesus had a need-satisfaction approach to His mission and ministry, it is very important to point out that He also performed many miracles to satisfy the needs of hurting people, without any call to discipleship. His ministry was characterized by compassion and disinterested benevolence towards all humanity. Jesus did good to people, not because it was good to do good, or because it was a useful tool to win them for His kingdom, but because He genuinely loved them and felt their pain. Ellen White observes, "during His ministry Jesus devoted more time to healing the sick than to preaching. His miracles testified to the truth of His words, that He came not to destroy but to save. His righteousness went before Him, and the glory of the Lord was His reward. Wherever He went, the tidings of His mercy preceded Him. Where He had passed, the objects of His compassion were rejoicing in health, and making trial of their new-found powers."[29]

Jesus is the great model of mission from the outside in, mission that targeted the felt and even unrecognized needs of people, awakening their hope and stimulating their faith to believe in Him as the Savior of the world. Ellen White admonishes, "the followers of Christ are to labor as He did. We are to feed the hungry, clothe the naked, and comfort the suffering and afflicted. We are to minister to the despairing, and inspire hope in the hopeless. . . . The love of Christ, manifested in unselfish ministry, will be more effective in reforming the evildoer than will the sword or the court of justice. . . . Often the heart will harden under reproof; but it will melt under the love of Christ."[30]

The goal of this book, therefore, is to help our leaders, pastors, and members in comprehending how a shift from an organization-centered to a people-centered orientation will benefit the mission of the church in the world. Firstly, a people-centered orientation in mission will take into consideration the contextual needs of the targeted audience. This will add more focus, relevance and power to the preaching from our pulpits, and to the ministries in our pews and communities. This orientation will encourage pastors to seek to understand the needs of the congregation (through visitation, questionnaires, pew cards, etc.) and tailor their sermons to address those needs. It will help pastors and leaders develop customer-value[31] consciousness, so that they will formulate their sermons and their services around the perceived values of their congregations and communities.

Consequently, pastoral sermons will be proclaimed from a sense of congregational needs, instead of the fancies of the pastor's own imagination. This type of preaching will give relevance to the Word from the pulpit, and meaning to the lives in the pews. For example, a sermon on Daniel in the lions' den can have as its take-home value "God Can Be Trusted". For a sermon on the state of the dead, the take-home value could be "We Have Hope." In this context, the central questions facing the pastor as he stands in the pulpit will be: What congregational needs am I going to address today? What value/s do I want my members to take home with them today? How-to or How-can-I sermons are excellent preaching tools to offer take-home value to church members.

Today's generations are looking for answers to the complex issues and problems that trouble them, and practical, value-based preaching, teaching, and application of the gospel are the best approaches that the servants of Christ can use to satisfy them. We must follow in the footsteps of the Master, who, after serving the hungry multitudes and His disciples a copious measure of His new wine (in the form of parables), privately instructed the twelve saying: "*Every scribe who has been trained for the kingdom of heaven is like the master of a household who brings out of his treasure what is new and what is old*" (Matthew 13:52 NRSV). It is the minister's responsibility to diligently search the treasure-house of God's word, unearth old truths, and formulate them in a new setting so that the word would be characterized with a freshness that will appeal to present-day hearers.

Ford motor company is still in the business of making Ford automobiles, but there is always a renewing of the form, appearance, features, and performance as the company endeavors to remain in touch with current trends. I am not prescribing that our ministers adopt a consumeristic approach to the gospel, but must rather be attuned to the forces that are shaping the thinking and experience of their congregations and local community and let the gospel come alive in addressing the concerns of both.

Essentially, what can be said of the pastor's sermon in terms of value offering can be said of every service the church offers its members and the local community. In this way, services and programs that target the local community will be evaluated in terms of the value they offer to the people being served. This will encourage the church to step out of itself and into the needs of the community for a better understanding of the services that people require.

From Internal Gazing to Strategic Thinking

Another major benefit of shifting the mission paradigm of the church towards a marketing orientation (people-centeredness) is that it will encourage church leaders and decision-makers to make the mental and emotional adjustment from the challenges associated with internal gazing and policy enforcing to the beckoning horizons identified with strategic planning and action. The complex, massive machinery that runs the Seventh-day Adventist Church is inundated with all types of policies that are geared to maintain internal control in order to ensure smooth organizational operation. Yet, while policies in themselves may not be bad, they tend to be internally focused, inequitably administered by those in authority, and often age and become irrelevant with the passing of time.

Moreover, since policies are geared toward more internal control, structural maintenance, and organizational efficiency, they tend to be less responsive to changes taking place in the environment outside of the organization. This slowness to respond to societal needs is compounded by the fact that within the church's organizational bureaucracy, decisions are made from the top down and can sometimes hinder the church's ability to capitalize on spur-of-the-moment ministry opportunities. Bill Hull complains that "our churches are not organized for growth and fulfilling their mission. The mission *must come first*, but in most contemporary churches, policy and rules come first, and these are organized for security, predictability, and safety"[32] (italics mine). I believe this phenomenon is very much a part of my church.

Hull further states that "the Pharisees' appetite for tradition stemmed from *their obsession with controlling the religious activity of Israel*. The threatened person is one who enjoys safeguards, who needs controls to limit variety. The Pharisaic tendency to weight the Jewish people with policy created a massive machinery that served as a major contributor to their stumbling over Jesus. Their traditions were protections from the new, the fresh, the creative, and, tragically, from the truth. The church often labors under much the same weighty machinery, thus causing it to miss new and effective means of fulfilling its mission"[33] (italics mine).

Is there any lesson here for us as God's chosen end-time people who are living on the verge of Jesus' second coming? Are we walking in the steps of the Pharisees, trying to control a massive bureaucracy by multiplying policies, while we stumble over the real purpose of our existence as a community of faith? The Seventh-day Adventist organizational system may be one of the most multilayered and multi-administrative church systems of modern times, and this phenomenon places considerable strain upon the church's financial resources, and on the efficiency of its decision-making processes. At the 1999 Annual Church Council in Brazil, George Knight pointed out that there is no church in the world with as many administrative levels to support as our church. We have even outdone the Roman Catholics, who have 2 levels above the local church, whereas we have 4.[34]

Knight also went on to make the very cogent observation that "more and more Adventists are realizing that there are other ways to structure the church in the post-modern world that would free up both workers and money for finishing God's work on earth. Too much money, claim many, is being used to run the machinery, as if it were an end in itself. Many of the potential opportunities of the future are contingent upon successfully restructuring in a manner that will free up resources and encourage the investment of additional resources. This task may be one of the greatest challenges of our day."[35]

We must come to grips with the fact that it places considerable stress on the system to pump financial resources from a solitary income base up four top-heavy levels of administration. This present situation is the reverse of what the early church pioneers intended for the Advent Movement, and many are left to wonder if the tail is wagging the dog, or the dog its tail—that is, whether the church exists for its administrative structure, or the structure for the church. Sooner not later, church leaders would have to make some very difficult decisions regarding administrative structures and services because financial constraints, precipitated by adverse economic conditions and membership dissatisfaction and apathy, will force them to do so.

As the church continues its rapid growth around

the world, there will always be the temptation to increase administrative structure for fear of losing control over people and resources, but Bill Hull thinks that this is a great fallacy. He says, "this bureaucratic pathology believes it is good to involve more and more people in administrative decision-making as the church grows. But the opposite is true! The larger an organization becomes, the more that administrative decisions should be delegated. The church should not broaden its administrative base, it should expand its ministry base. It must streamline its structures by removing administrative layers, reducing the number of committees, shrinking the time involved in administration, and limiting the number of decision-makers."[36]

I would like to encourage the leaders and people of God's church to take up the very promising challenge of pursuing the task of mission and ministry from a strategic standpoint, and allow the mission of the church to be the immovable compass that gives direction with regard to organizational structure, ministries, and programs. When we combine this approach with a market-oriented worldview, we may not even begin to imagine the growth or success possibilities that would be open to the church. This is not to say that the growth and success of the church will be totally dependent on the type of strategies we bring to bear on the work. However, when we offer to God our best human efforts, coupled with the blessing of His Spirit, we can and will accomplish greater exploits for Him. Ellen White comments:

1. "The secret of success is the union of divine power

with human effort."[37]

2. "Human effort avails nothing without divine power, and without human endeavor, divine effort is with many of no avail."[38]

3. "If a man has tact, industry, and enthusiasm, he will make a success in temporal business, and the same qualities, consecrated to the work of God, will prove even doubly efficient; for divine power will be combined with human effort."[39] In all our endeavors we must remember, "we are laborers *together* with God" (1 Cor 3:9, emphasis mine).

In his amalgamation of marketing management and strategic planning, Kotler describes the resulting combination in the following way: "Market-oriented strategic planning is the managerial process of developing and maintaining a viable fit between the organization's objectives, skills, and resources and its changing market opportunities. The aim of strategic planning is to shape and reshape the company's businesses and products so that they yield target profits and growth."[40] In the context of the church, this means matching a ministry's skills and resources with environmental opportunities in order to accomplish the church's objectives and fulfill its mission. Migliore and others say that "the objective of this process is to peer through the 'strategic window' (an opportunity that will not always be there) and identify opportunities which the individual church or ministry is equipped to take advantage of or respond to."[41]

Essentially, a strategic orientation is externally focused, placing emphasis on responsiveness and adaptability with regard to changes in the business or even social environment. With this orientation, the church's mission will determine its organizational structure, services, and programming. Since the ultimate goal of the mission is saving lost people, and the marketing approach to mission is rooted in the philosophy of synergistically relating the gospel to the felt and un-felt needs[42] of these people, the typical organizational structure of the church should resemble the one illustrated in figure 1. This is the *upside down kingdom philosophy*.[43] The chiefs shall be servants indeed, and not laud it over their subjects.

Figure 1

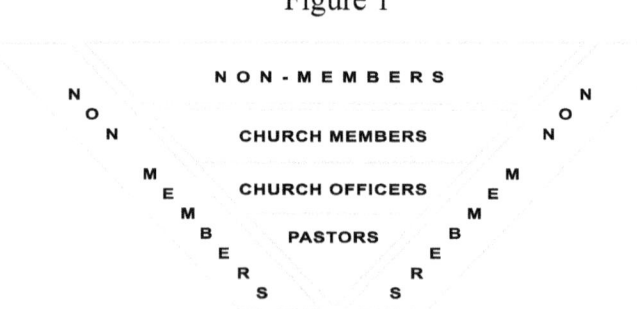

Figure 1. Strategic Church Organizational Chart Adapted from Bill Marriott's (Chairman of Marriott Hotels) "The 'Correct' View of the Chart Company Organization," quoted by Philip Kotler, *Marketing Management* (Englewood Cliffs, NJ: Prentice Hall, 1994), 23.

SHIFTING OUR MISSION PARADIGM

In this structure, the non-members (both Christians and non-Christians) are the most important group of people (in terms of mission objectives), who need to hear and respond to a clear presentation of the everlasting gospel. These are the people who give the church a reason for its existence in the world. Next in the order of priority, are the front-line people (church members), who meet, serve, and attempt to establish caring, working relationships with these non-members. Below these are our middle managers (church officers), whose job it is to support the church members so that they can properly serve their non-Adventist friends and neighbors. And finally, at the base is our top management (pastors), whose job it is to equip and support church officers, so that they, in turn, can equip and support our church members, who make all the difference in whether the non-Adventist community feels satisfied with the products and services of the Seventh-day Adventist Church.

It is also very important to observe in this model that the other Christian and non-Christian target groups are also at the sides of the above figure, in order to indicate that all the church members, officers, and pastors are personally involved in knowing, meeting, and serving non-members. In this entire scenario, the church's strategic decision-making process will be formulated in the context of (1) its operating environment, (2) its purpose and mission, and (3) its mission objectives. These will be explored in greater detail in chapter 6. This simple model may be a healthy starting point for church leaders as they grapple with the very difficult issue of restructuring the larger church organization for growth and efficiency.

Additionally, people-oriented strategic planning will do much to strengthen membership conservation efforts within the Adventist community and will also help to enhance the service and image of the church around the world. Philip Kotler has rightly said, "Satisfied customers remain loyal longer, buy more, are less cost sensitive, and talk favorably about the company."[44] This fact also holds true for the church: Satisfied church members will probably remain loyal to church longer, are most likely to invest more in the cause of Christ, and will be more likely to talk favorably about Christ and the church. Herein lies a possible solution for the volunteer fallout problem facing the church. Kotler hits home on this very point when he writes: "It always costs more to attract new customers than to retain current customers. Therefore, *customer retention* is more critical than *customer attraction*. The key to customer retention is *customer satisfaction*. . . . Delighted customers are more effective advertisers than all the paid advertisements placed in the media."[45]

In this regard, he says that there are at least four important steps[46] that an organization needs to take to reduce member defection:

1. The organization must define and measure its retention rate. For the church, this could be the membership (or even missing member) count per year.

2. The organization must distinguish the various

causes of customer attrition and identify those that can be managed better. Instead of guessing why members leave, the church can possibly interview these members (via personal visitation) and prepare a frequency distribution to show the percentage of members who defect for different reasons.

3. The organization needs to estimate how much profit it loses when it loses customers unnecessarily. In the case of the church, this may be very difficult to calculate, since we cannot place a price tag on souls, or accurately measure the real and potential losses to the church and society in terms of the displaced talents and gifts of these former members. We may be able to calculate our losses in terms of the tithe and offerings of former members, but we cannot even begin to measure what the aggregate losses would be once these people leave the fellowship of the church: for example, (a) the potential loss of a soul for whom Christ has died; (b) the losses caused by their negative publicity regarding the church; and (c) their potential to inflict great pain and suffering upon the church in the future. Ellen White hints, "As the storm approaches, . . . men of talent and pleasing address, who once rejoiced in the truth, employ their powers to deceive and mislead souls. They become the most bitter enemies of their former brethren."[47]

4. The organization needs to determine how much it would cost to reduce the defection rate. The cost to the church should not really be a factor here, since we are not dealing with bottom-line issues, per se, but the eternal worth of a human soul. If the God of heaven would expend the best

gifts at His disposal (Jesus Christ, the Holy Spirit, and the angels) to save one lost soul, how could the body that bears the marks and name of His only Son do any less?

In the world of business, there has been a major paradigm shift in the way modern companies relate to their customers, and there is so much that the church can learn from this. In the classical marketing approach, companies used to place their emphasis on creating transactions (just making a sale), rather than forming a relationship (having a repeat or loyal customer).[48] This is very much like the church that places emphasis on creating baptisms rather than on forming strong, caring relationships that anchor converts in the love of Jesus Christ and the service of the church.

Discussion focuses on pre-sale and sale activities—what we can do to have another sale, rather than on post-sale activity—how can we bond with our customers to keep them coming back for more? Similarly, some churches spend more time discussing how to get more souls into the baptismal pool than on how to form genuine redemptive relationships with the unsaved and to make them fruitful disciples of Jesus Christ. In response to administrative pressure, many pastors labor under the load of trying to add numbers to their baptismal count (sale approach), instead of bringing potential disciples into genuine relationships with Christ for the advancement of His kingdom.

Today, however, more and more companies are recognizing the importance of retaining current customers, and have turned their attention to building long-term relationships with them through relationship marketing. How true is Jesus' statement that "in their generation the children of this world are wiser than the children of light" (Luke 11:8 KJV).

This is a very good example through which the children of the Kingdom may learn some important lessons from the children of the world. I believe we can strengthen our membership conservation efforts if we can move leadership and the church in the direction of relationship marketing. Such a move will focus mission and ministry, not so much on the number of persons being baptized (even though this is very important and cannot be lost sight of), but on making disciples[49] through long-term, caring relationships that are rooted in the compassionate love of Jesus Christ.

We must also remember that the church operates, for the most part, on volunteer service, and that these people all have needs just as the people they serve. When needs of believers are carefully serviced through the various ministries, small groups, and human resource development programs in the church, burnout and fallout problems can be (if at all) very limited. In other words, the church must become more adept with regard to external and internal marketing—that is, the art of making and keeping disciples.

However, I must offer a word of caution here. While customer-oriented thinking and planning will ultimately influence the packaging and presentation of the Advent message, leaders of the church must be encouraged and guided in maintaining integrity to the core principles and requirements of the gospel. This is not to say that the gospel or the standards of the church should be diluted to suit the whims and fancies of this secular age, but that the form of presentation must be relevant to the needs of modern man. Dan Day elaborates on this very point: "The issue is not whether or not we change our beliefs or re-organize our church. It's whether or not we've understood our customers' needs well enough to show how what we have matches what they need. The key is how honestly and totally we're committed to meeting the needs of the people Jesus called us to reach."[50]

We must not become guilty of scratching where there is no itch—that is, providing answers to questions people are not even asking. It is, by far, more productive to scratch where it does itch, or create the itch for our scratching. Ellen G. White said, "men are needed who pray to God for wisdom, and who, under the guidance of God, can put *new life into the old methods of labor and can invent new plans and new methods of awakening the interest of church members and reaching the men and women of the world*"[51] (italics mine). The time for such men is long overdue, for the church urgently needs those new plans and methods if it ever hopes to make a meaningful impact in a skeptical world. We must always remember that we occupy a unique position in this world for one purpose—to serve people. We were also given a special end-time message for a specific reason—that is, to warn the world of its impending doom, and to reach the *people* of every nation, tribe and language, with the everlasting gospel of Jesus Christ.

The church, in its mission assignment, has been mandated to be people-oriented (or customer-oriented) and must therefore seek to understand the needs of the "publics" it serves and design its ministries to satisfy those needs. This customer-oriented perspective will help to reinforce the church's mission offensive, promote Christian fellowship and brotherhood, and reduce the gross insularism that is hurting the witness of the church in different parts of the world. John Stott observed, "unless we listen attentively to the voices of secular society, unless we struggle to understand them, unless we feel with modern men and women in their frustration, their alienation, their pain and even sometimes, their despair, I think we shall lack authenticity as the followers of Jesus of Nazareth."[52]

Quite often in our mission approach, we become so pre-occupied with the dispensing of our pre-packaged message that we seldom take time to listen to, or hear, the concerns of secular people. We operate more from a preaching/teaching mode than from a listening mode. This approach tends to pre-judge the target audience and treat it as a homogenous unit. It is no wonder, therefore, that our message sometimes misses the intended target. However, if we approach mission and ministry from a marketing perspective, it will help us to suspend judgment regarding non-Adventists (Christians or unbelievers) and will place us in a mode that seeks for understanding through active listening, thus increasing our chances of making the gospel more relevant to the hearers.

Present world conditions demand that, as true followers of Jesus Christ, we must be committed to changing the face of Adventist global mission. We must be committed to incorporating the mind and character of Christ in the very heart of our mission process and practice. Like her Master, God's remnant church must become known not only as a people with a message for the end-time, but also as a Christian community whose ontological experience is characterized by a daily pursuit to love and serve all people. This commitment will be self-evident in the way that that community of faith relates socially, cross-culturally, inter-culturally, and ethnically within the body of Christ. Let us endeavor to make every Adventist community of faith a reflection of the *outside in, upside down Kingdom* of Jesus Christ.

Notes

1. Wright, 32.
2. Martin Seeley, "Asking 'Why' Questions Now," *Management and Ministry*, ed. John Nelson (Norfolk, England: Canterbury Press Norwich, 1996), 171.
3. Wade Clark Roof, *Spiritual Marketplace: Baby Boomers and the Remaking of American Religion* (Princeton, N.J.: Princeton University Press, 1999), 8.
4. Martin E. Marty, "Where the Energies Go," *Annals of the American Academy of Political and Social Science 527* (May 1993): 11-26.
5. Richard N. Ostling, "America's Ever-Changing Religious Landscape: Where We've Come From and Where We're Going," *Brookings Review* (Spring 1999): 13.
6. For a full discussion of this subject see White, *Desire of Ages*, 31-38.

7. Ibid.
8. Ibid. 279.
9. Bill Hull, *Revival that Reforms* (Grand Rapids: Fleming H. Revell, 1998), 101.
10. George Barna, *The Frog and the Kettle*, 223.
11. White, *Evangelism*, 105.
12. Ibid., 104-105.
13. Robert G. Lee, *How to Lead a Soul to Christ* (Grand Rapids: Zondervan Publishing House, 1955), 30.
14. White, *Testimony to the Church* 9:189-90.
15. G. Ralph Thompson spoke these words as part of his keynote address to the delegates and visitors at the Adventist World Session 2000, in Toronto Canada, on July 1, 2000.
16. Darill L. Guder ed., *Missional Church: A Vision for the Sending of the Church in North America* (Grand Rapids, MI: Wm. B. Eerdmans, 1998), 20.
17. Words of Dietrich Bonhoeffer were quoted in George G. Hunter III, *Church for the Unchurched* (Nashville: Abingdon Press, 1996), 24.
18. Donald Miller, *Reinventing American Protestantism* (Berkeley, CA: University of California Press, 1997), 18.
19. Leith Anderson, *Dying for Change* (Minneapolis: Bethany House Publishers, 1990), 117.
20. Ralph Neighbor, *Where Do We Go From Here?* (Houston, Touch Publications, 1990), 36.
21. Peter Drucker, lecture at Leadership Network, September 1991, quoted in Bill Hull, *7 Steps to Transform Your Church* (Grand Rapids: Fleming H. Revell, 1993), 101.
22. George G. Hunter III, *Church for the Unchurched*, 24-25.
23. This Swiss watchmaker illustration was adapted from Joel Barker, *Future Edge* (New York: William Morrow, 1992), 15-19.
24. James Emery White, *Rethinking the Church: A Challenge to Creative Redesign in and Age of Transition* (Grand Rapids: Baker Book, 1997), 21.
25. Bill Hull, *7 Steps to Transform Your Church* (Grand Rapids: Fleming H. Revell, 1993), 101-102.
26. Webster, 33.
27. Ellen White, *Desire of Ages,* 194.
28. Dan Day, *A Guide to Marketing Adventism* (Boise, ID: Pacific Press Publishing Association, 1990), 16.
29. White, *Desire of Ages*, 350.
30. Ibid.
31. Value is the consumer's estimate of the product's/service's overall capacity to satisfy his or her needs. Kotler, 8.
32. Hull, *7 Steps to Transform Your Church*, 102.

33. Hull, *Jesus Christ, DiscipleMaker*, 106.
34. George Knight, "If I Were the Devil." Sermon presented at Adventist World Session 2000, Toronto Canada on July 2, 2000.
35. Ibid.
36. Bill Hull, *7 Steps to Transform Your Church*, 103.
37. White, *Patriarchs and Prophets*, 509.
38. White, *Prophets and Kings* (Mountain View, CA: Pacific Press Publishing Association, 1943), 486.
39. White, *Testimonies for the Church* 5: 276.
40. Kotler, 62
41. R Henry Migliore and others, *Church and Ministry Strategic Planning: From Concept to Success* (Binghamton, NY: The Haworth Press, Inc., 1994), 20.
42. Felt needs are those needs that are most present in the mind of the lost and not the mind of the Christian observer. Un-felt needs are those needs that are very real but not quite obvious to the person possessing them. These needs are often fleshed out by the power of the gospel and the influence of the Holy Spirit. Eg. A secular person may have a felt need for finding a job, but may also possess an un-felt (or un-realized) need for forgiveness and peace.
43. See Mark 10:42-45.
44. Kotler, 59.
45. Ibid. 20-21.
46. Ibid. 47.
47. Ellen White, *The Faith I Live By* (Washington, DC: Review and Herald Publishing Association, 1973), 336.
48. Kotler, 47.
49. The focus here is on relational discipleship, and not just on church membership.
50. Dan Day, 16.
51. White, *Evangelism*, 105.
52. John Stott, "Secular Challenges to the Contemporary Church," *Crux* (September, 1991): 2.

6

MARKET SENSITIVE MISSION AND MINISTRY

"*M*inistry is not about programs. Ministry is [all] about people... and it happens when a person's needs are met."[1] Hull says that we must "always remember that the real business of the Church is people—not policies, procedures, or politics."[2] This is the essence of mission and ministry relevance. It is the ability of people (or organizations) to ascertain the needs of a target audience by listening to, or asking, the relevant questions, and to strategically assemble and coordinate all their available resources to facilitate ongoing beneficial exchanges with that audience.

Operating in this mode, people (or organizations) are prone to be more responsive to the needs of the target population and are more disposed to tailor their offerings—that is, services or programs—to relate to those needs. Barna says, "a market-driven church will be people-centered, not program centered. It will develop ministries to solve problems, rather than expecting people to force their problems into some preset ministry mold. Ministry will be an interactive, evolving process, not a static structure in which everything can be foreseen and handled via organizational procedures."[3] Kotler and Levy made this very important statement: "For an organization to remain viable, its management must provide for periodic audits of its objectives, resources, and opportunities. It must reexamine its basic business, target groups, differentiate advantage, communication channels, and messages in the light of current trends and needs."[4]

All these activities suggested by Kotler and Levy are interrelated functions that operate within the strategic marketing planning process and, along with some other key concepts, I will apply them to the work and mission of the Seventh-day Adventist Church. While I do not share Barna's belief that the Church should be market-driven in order to be a viable organization that would engage modern society, I do believe that the church should be aware of, and take into consideration, the needs of the masses that throng the market-place as it plans and executes its mission. In other words the church must be *market-sensitive*, but *totally and completely mission-driven*. Ministry and the market-place are inseparable mission stations; for ministry always lead to the market-place.

In this regard, I would like to introduce a managerial concept that I believe would help church leaders keep the issue of the church's mission central and fully operative. In the world of business, "Management By Objectives" (MBO) is a very popular concept that has aided managers to guide their organizations to entrepreneurial success. Gregory Moorehead and Ricky W. Griffin define "Management By Objectives" as "a collaborative goal-setting process through which organizational goals systematically filter down through the organization."⁵ In this way, organizational goals are shared and known at every level of the organization. In the realm of the church, MBO (which I choose to reinterpret "Mission/Ministry By Objectives") can be a very useful tool to motivate and help church leaders fulfill the goals of the organization.

Douglas Webster raised two very important questions that deserve honest, objective answers by church leaders today. "If we're in the business of reaching people for Christ, why not take marketing strategies that have been proven successful among baby boomers and use them to help motivate this powerful and influential target audience to buy into the Christian faith? If polls and surveys tell us what turns Americans on, what's wrong with using that knowledge to turn the keys of the kingdom?"⁶ My honest answer to Douglas is "I don't know," but it surely conjures up in my mind Jesus' statement regarding the wisdom of the dishonest steward in Luke 16:1-13 NRSV: "And his master commended the dishonest manager because he had acted shrewdly; *for the children of this age are more shrewd in dealing with their own generation than are the children of light*" (italics mine).

The point for us here is that Jesus applauded the wisdom of the servant, but not the application the servant made of it. If the servant was faithful in his handling of his master's goods, he could have used his wisdom in a more honest and positive way. I am of the opinion that the children of light can use their God-given wisdom to apply the very useful body of knowledge provided through marketing management to turn the keys of the kingdom.

Strategic Mission/Ministry[7] Planning Process – Part I

Simply stated, strategic planning involves the matching and utilization of an organization's resources in response to opportunities that arise in the environment. These opportunities develop over time, and decisions must be made as to whether or not the organization's resources should be used to address them. While there are many different ways the church could choose to pursue the strategic mission planning process, a simple, systematic approach, based on a series of predetermined questions,[8] would provide the church with step by step guidelines for accomplishing its objectives. For example:

1. What are we going to do? This will bring focus on specific needs that the church will try to address.

2. Whom are we doing this for? This will identify the target population whose needs will be addressed.

3. How are we going to accomplish this? This question challenges church leaders to focus their attention on the different avenues through which the stated needs may be served.

The basic framework that can guide church leaders in strategic decision-making is (1) the Church's operating environment, (2) the Church's purpose or mission statement, and (3) the Church's mission objectives.[9] Kotler and Andreasen[10] have done an excellent job on expanding this framework, and I have chosen to adopt and apply this to the mission and ministry of the church. The successful application of this strategic mission decision framework may require church leaders and members to get help from someone within the organization who is adept at religious marketing or strategic planning (if such a one exists), or better still, hire an outside marketing expert with a strong religious orientation. If the leadership chooses to use someone from within the organization, precautions should be taken that the marketing or strategic planning process and results would not be subjected to extreme organizational bias.

In this section, I will outline and explain a few core principles that characterize strategic market planning, so that church leaders and members may have an idea of the range of possibilities available to them if they wisely apply these principles to the task of mission and ministry. I will also attempt to reformulate some of the marketing jargon so that it reflects a mission/ministry perspective in its application to the issues presented in this discussion. It is not my intention, however, to make these principles hard-and-fast rules for doing mission and ministry, for their application will change as the mission environment changes. However, I am recommending them as a basic framework to stimulate further investigation, experimentation and, possibly, further amplification.

Analyze the Church as an Organization

The analysis of the church as an organization should include an examination of its culture, mission, goals, objectives, strengths and weaknesses. Every organization has its unique operating culture, which represents the underlying assumptions and unspoken expectations that influence the way things are done within the organization. Seventh-day Adventism has its own unique vocabulary, dress code, unspoken rules of conduct and expectations, and extraordinary lifestyle. Commenting on the corporate culture that contributes to the success of their "best-run" organizations, Peters and Waterman offer the following insight: "Without exception, the dominance and coherence of culture proved to be an essential quality of the excellent companies. *Moreover, the stronger the culture and the more it was directed toward the marketplace, the less need was there for policy manuals, organization charts, or detailed procedures and rules.* In these companies, people, way down the line, know what they are supposed to do in most situations because the handful of guiding values is crystal clear"[11] (italics mine).

No doubt a customer-centered orientation can be very useful in enhancing the corporate culture of the Seventh-day Adventist church. Therefore, in the strategic planning process, church leaders must be prepared to take a candid look at the church's corporate culture to see how well it is aligned to the overall mission, present goals, and objectives of the church. Moreover, the church's mission, goals and objectives should be clearly defined, communicated, understood and owned not only by church leaders, but by the members as well.

1. Mission: This describes the church's purpose and reason for its existence in a particular community—that is, why do we exist? What are we to be as a church? What does God want us to do for this community and the world as a church? How are we to do it?[12] Pastors and church officers can lead their congregations in defining the purposes of the church in the local community, and once these purposes are discovered, the church's ministries and programs should be organized around them. Rick Warren, pastor of the Saddleback Church in southern California suggests that the purpose-driven church should be committed to the five tasks that Christ ordained for His church—namely, (1) love the Lord with all your heart (commitment to worship), (2) love your neighbor as yourself (commitment to ministry), (3) go and make disciples (commitment to evangelism), (4) baptize them (commitment to community and fellowship), and (5) teach them to obey (commitment to discipleship).[13] Kotler suggests that an organization should strive for a mission that is *feasible, motivating, and distinctive.*[14]

2. Goal: A specific objective stated in an operational and measurable form—e.g. establishing 3 branch Sabbath-schools in the first six months of the year, or increasing our visitors attendance to worship service by 20 persons per week, or baptizing 100 persons by the end of the year.

3. Objective: This may be a major area of focus or accomplishment the church would like to target. The focus could be any, or all, of the five tasks mentioned above under the mission heading—for example, creating a worship atmosphere that would attract more visitors to the church.

The church must also make a careful reassessment of its strengths and weaknesses as they relate to the total resources (people, finance, skills and talents, fixed assets - buildings, land etc.) available for use in the pursuit of its mission objective and goals. To accomplish this, church leaders should perform periodic audits, not only of finances, but of all areas of church operations. This involves a comprehensive, systematic, independent, and periodic examination of the church's mission environment, objectives, strategies, and activities, with the specific view of determining problem areas and opportunities, and recommending a plan of action to improve the church's strategic mission performance.[15] For an organizational audit to be of any productive use, it must be governed by the four characteristics identified above:

4. Comprehensive: The organizational audit must cover all the major mission issues facing the church, both within and without the organization.

5. Systematic: The audit should involve an orderly sequence of diagnostic steps covering the church's mission environment, internal mission system, and specific mission activities. The diagnosis is followed by a corrective action plan that covers both short and long-term proposals to

MARKET SENSITIVE MISSION AND MINISTRY

improve the church's mission effectiveness.

6. Independent: The audit should be conducted by a capable individual, who has sufficient independence from the church, to facilitate its objectivity and integrity.

7. Periodic: The audit should be conducted periodically and not only in a time of crisis. This will help to keep the church on track regarding its mission and probably avert any crisis that may be lurking on the horizon.

Based on my experience as a minister and as a strategic planning professional, I believe that an organizational audit will greatly benefit the local congregation and the higher organization, enhancing the overall mission operations of the church as a whole. Two areas within the Adventist community that I view can readily profit from such an audit are: (1) Church structure and decision-making process, and (2) Approach to mission and ministry.

Church Structure and Decision-making Process

Since the local church is the last level on the Seventh-day Adventist five-tiered organizational structure,[16] it is rather easy for it to become a victim of the decision-making process. Most organizational decisions are filtered down through the organization chain before they reach the local church, and sometimes they are not timely or even relevant to the local church situation. Often local churches feel imposed upon when decisions are made about them without their input and without regard to what's going on in the community of faith at the time.

As a pastor, I can recall incidents of having to shelve the program of the local church, because the Conference, and sometimes the Union, had something else on their agenda—for example, an unscheduled crusade by some visiting evangelist, an unplanned departmental workshop, or some other program promotion. I can also remember the confusion and disarray among the churches that resulted when the General Conference (GC) made the decision to merge several organizational departments under one head called "Church Ministries Department." This may not have been a bad decision by the GC, but it was certainly not a shared decision in many areas of the World Church. It may be a very good idea for leadership in the organizational hierarchy to take a periodic look at the structure of the organization and its decision-making process, and see if steps can be taken to increase overall organizational efficiency and effectiveness. Such an effort may require organizational audit.

One option that is a major buzzword in the corporate world, and to some degree in many mainline denominations, is a process called organizational re-engineering. Hammer and Champy describe this process as "the *fundamental* rethinking and *radical* redesign of business *process* to achieve *dramatic* improvements in critical, contemporary measures of performance, such as cost, quality, service, and speed"[17] (italics mine). In this definition, there are four important words that need our earnest consideration:

1. <u>Fundamental</u>: This requires asking the most basic

questions about our church or organization, and how we operate. Why do we do what we do? And why do we do it the way we do?

Asking these fundamental questions will force us to look at the tacit rules, policies, and assumptions that underlie the way we conduct our business of managing churches and carrying out mission. Often these rules and policies turn out to be obsolete, erroneous, or even inappropriate.[18] This is a common situation in many churches today. I have seen church officers going through rounds of the same activity year, after year, after year. Then others succeed them and do exactly what they saw their predecessors do. Hardly anyone stops to ask, why are we doing this the way we do? The general posture seems to suggest: "Well, this got me through last year, and I'll just go right ahead and do the same thing again this year."

2. Radical: Hammer and Champy suggest that the etymology of the word (Latin *"radix"* meaning "root") requires the organization to get to the root of things: not just making superficial changes or fiddling with what is already in place, but throwing away the old.[19] Radical redesign means disregarding all existing structures and procedures and inventing completely new ways of accomplishing the work. Howard Snyder suggests, "for a radical gospel (the biblical kind) we need a radical church (the biblical kind). For the ever-new wine we must continually have new wineskins."[20]

When I first read this, I uttered the proverbial "Wow!" "This is indeed revolutionary!" "This is really heavy stuff!"

"My church needs this!" However, when the cold reality set in, I immediately realized that organizational re-engineering may be a very tall order for the Seventh-day Adventist Church. Besides having to deal with denominational pride, the structural inertia of vested interest, and the paralyzing fear of change, there are just too many "sacred cows" to slay along the way. But church-historian George Knight would have us remember, "the 1861-1863 and 1901-1903 organizational structures were not divinely inspired, but were established to facilitate mission."[21]

However, a gnawing question continues to nibble at my brain: If the people in the business world could be so much in earnest about what they do, that they are willing to radically redesign an entire organization in order to achieve a desired, but mundane end, how really serious are we about finishing the *Missio Dei* and hastening the return of Jesus? Leading organizational theorist, Colin Hastings, had this to say about traditional organizations: "The way that we organize our enterprises and public bodies has remained essentially unchanged for several thousand years. Perhaps more importantly, the way we picture organizations in our minds and the way we think about how they work is deeply ingrained in every one of us. Which is why, when this traditional way of organizing begins to let us down, begins to show its inability to deal with quite momentous levels of change, we all find it difficult to see alternatives, let alone comprehend or implement them."[22]

Church growth specialist, C. Peter Wagner,

comments, "denominational structures that worked only a couple of decades ago are now becoming obsolete. God is pouring out new wine, and many old wineskins are proving dysfunctional. A call for renewal of the old wineskins will be inadequate in most cases. Only a determination for 'reinventing' or 're-engineering,' which means, to all intents and purposes, starting from scratch, may prove to be a viable solution."[23]

My hope is that some aspect of this re-engineering concept will hit home with church leaders and challenge them with the possibilities of casting new vision for mission and ministry on the landscape of Adventism.

3. Dramatic: Re-engineering is not about making marginal or incremental improvements but about achieving quantum leaps in performance. It should be brought in only when the need exists for heavy blasting. Marginal improvements require fine-tuning; dramatic improvement demands blowing up the old and replacing it with something new.[24]

This type of language may strike fear in the hearts of people who spend all their lives trying to protect and preserve an organization, because their livelihood depends on it. On the other hand, re-engineering may ring a bell of hope in the heart of others who are in dead earnest about finishing the mission that the organization was created to accomplish and moving on to something else. The world and, more so, the church need the latter, for both are conducting business in a time of crisis.

In his chapter on the "Five Dilemmas in the Institutionalization of Religion," Thomas O'Dea explains that genuine organizational reform becomes threatening to the status, security, and self-validation of the incumbents of office, because of mixed motivation that characterizes the bureaucracy.[25] This could well be the issue facing the Seventh-day Adventist Church when it comes to organizational reform. Now is not a time for fine-tuning the old form of yesteryear, which we have been doing for many years. Now is the time for heavy blasting, and we dare not just sit around and wait for the latter rain to do it. We must rise up and hasten that glad day.

4. <u>Processes</u>: This is the most difficult part of re-engineering, because most people are not "process-oriented"; they are focused on tasks, on jobs, on people, on structures, but not on process.[26] This concept has direct application to the work of the Seventh-day Adventist Church, since mission and ministry are very task-oriented. Even the name given to the missionary arm of the Church is "Lay Activities," which is very suggestive of a preoccupation with the work of Christ. This is extremely important and certainly must continue, but the focus of re-engineering is to make sure the processes involved in planning, facilitating, and engaging in mission, are smooth, efficient, and most of all, Christ-centered.

Many congregations go through the same yearly round of activities without giving any serious thought to even refining the processes that make the church and its mission operational. Kallestad's suggestion to such churches is to "reflect on ways to re-engineer the structure of your church so that your congregation can move from gridlock to effectiveness. Think of ways that you might move more quickly, with much greater confidence than ever before. A church is far more than its structure, but structure is hardly unimportant. A dysfunctional structure can paralyze a church."[27]

In an effort to help churches deal with the re-engineering process, Barna drafted a suggested change chart (fig. 2.) that can prove very helpful to church leaders around the world. He states that the "net effect of the changes will be to make the church more responsive and pro-active, without jeopardizing the core values and truths upon which the church is based. Structures, formats, styles, and relationships can be adapted to fit the church's goals and standards, regardless of past prohibitions and the existing expectations held by many people."[28]

Figure 2

Change factor:	Changing from:	Changing to:
Authority	centralized	decentralized
Leadership	pastor-driven	lay-driven
Power distribution	vertical	horizontal
Reaction to change	resistance	acceptance
Identity	tradition and order	mission and vision
Scope of ministry	all-purpose	specialized

Practices	tradition bound	relevance bound
People's role	observation and support	participation and innovation
Principal product	knowledge	transformation
Success factors	size, efficiency, image	accessibility, impact, integrity
Primary challenges	momentum, relationships, leadership, complacency	heresy, relationships, unity, leadership, balance
Effect of technology	attention-grabbing	growth-facilitating
Means to growth	more, better-run programs	more relationships and experience
Growth prospects	limited	unlimited

Figure 2. Change Chart for Re-engineering the Local Church. Source: *The Second Coming of the Church*, by George Barna, p. 177.

Approach to Mission and Ministry

Mission and ministry follow the traditional pattern of being centered around programs, formatted by the higher organization (Conference, Union, Division, and sometimes the General Conference), which is very often out of touch with what is happening at the local church level or in the external mission environment. I believe the days for one-size-fits-all programs are over, and the local church should be given some measure of autonomy to formulate its own programs or, at least, to make adjustment to the filtered-down models so that they can be relevant to the local mission situation. Mission and ministry should revolve around the needs of the community of faith and the needs of society, and not simply around programs that the higher organization is trying to funnel through the system.

James Emery White has accurately portrayed the typical approach to Adventist ministry. He says that the traditional approach to ministry is (1) Begin with a program, (2) Find some people, (3) Sell the program, (4) Carry out the program, (5) Maintain the program.[29] This is the approach that has characterized our ministry over the years. Warren writes: "Instead of trying to grow a church with programs, focus on growing people with a process. This concept is the heart of being a purpose-driven church. If you will set up a process for developing disciples and stick with it, your church's growth will be healthy, balanced, and consistent."[30]

To give an illustration of the process at the Saddleback Church, Warren says: "We bring people in, build them up, train them, and send them out. We bring them in as *members*, we build them up to *maturity*, we train them for *ministry*, and we send them out on *mission, magnifying* the Lord in the process. That's it! This is our total focus at Saddleback. We don't do anything else."[31]

This is a great story, and worthy of emulation, for it cuts right to the heart of what mission is about. The illustration clearly portrays the centrality of mission as the anchor to the entire process of bringing, building, training, and sending people. It is the hub of the total machinery of the Church. The illustration also focuses on the importance of people as the reason for and the goal of mission. It portrays a never-ending circle of activity involving people—that is, bring people, build people, train people, and send people to bring more people, and the process goes on.

Programs do have a place in mission and ministry, but too often they are leaned upon as crutches, when Christians would rather shun the hard work of brainstorming and creating their own programs around the needs of the local community. Canned programs tend to quench creativity of the gifted people in the community of faith, and are quite often out of touch with the needs of the people they are targeted to service. James Emery White says, "the most effective ministries in churches are those that are based on the knowledge of the needs and interests of the people a church is trying to minister to."[32]

Analyze the Church's External Environment

The church should have a clear understanding of the "publics" (internal and external) it intends to serve, its competition, and its macro-environment (social, political, technical, and economic). In this context, some form of market research should be done in order for the church to fathom and address the diversified needs of these publics—for example, Conference, officers, members, institutions, local community, etc. Aaker and Day say, "marketing research links the organization with its market environment. It involves the *specification, gathering, analyzing,* and *interpretation* of information to help management understand the environment, identify problems and opportunities, and develop and evaluate courses of marketing action."[33] This process involves the systematic and objective gathering of information for assisting managers in making decisions regarding a marketing situation facing the organization. The major steps associated with the research process are defining the problem and the research objectives, developing the research plan, collecting the information, analyzing the information, and presenting the findings.[34] Using this marketing tool, church leaders will be able to zero in on not only congregational needs, but the needs of the community as well.

Analyzing the external environment will also give church leaders and members a more informed understanding of who or what is their competition. For many, many years we have regarded other Christian denominations as our primary competition, and the non-Christian community only in a secondary sense. We have tried and, in many cases, succeeded in outmaneuvering and beating other Protestant denominations on the evangelistic battlefield, but how productive have been our victories? Have we been really tearing down the strongholds of Satan? While we compete with the other Protestant brothers and sisters, Satan is waging a one-sided war in many of our neighborhoods with drugs, all forms of sexual promiscuity, gang activity, and anti-social behaviors.

Who is our competition really? While other denominations may cherish beliefs different from ours, and some major elements of our mission are diametrically opposed to theirs, we must look for common (not competing) ground by which we could work with them to build up the kingdom of God. Admittedly, we tend to relate to other denominations as our major competitors, and often react to religious and communal practices in those communities, but, as I have already indicated in chapter 3, our main competition is any organization, opportunity, and philosophy that provide people with an alternative to the Christian life.

We are living in the information age, and those who control the information wield a mighty source of power. Our church members, and young people in particular, are exposed to a proliferation of information on all sides, and I do not believe that they are equipped and ready to filter off all that is coming at them. We cannot afford to sit back and just offer our members, and a mesmerized world, dry, reheated programs and services of yesteryear, and expect a faithful following. The merchants of this world are in dead earnest to win the confidence and the loyalty of the masses to buy into their offerings, regardless of how ridiculous and ungodly they may appear to be. They are serving up goods in very delightful styles and in a variety of places, and their aim is to win at all costs. We must also be in earnest about our mission and ministry to the lost. We must be constrained to use all the resources at our disposal to find creative and productive ways to relate to the needs and interests of members and non-members alike. Barna says, "if we hope to include people in the life of the church, we must provide appealing and high quality activities that can successfully compete for people's time, attention and resources."[35]

It is also important for church leaders to understand the social and political arena in which they have to operate, and to keep abreast with the economic and technological changes taking place in and around them. While the internal environment will inform church leaders of what is desired and permissible, the external environment will tell them what is possible.

The information and knowledge gained from environmental analyses can then be integrated to set strategic mission objectives and goals. This process will involve the coordinating of information to determine what long-term course of marketing action would best achieve the church's organizational mission and objectives. This marketing mission may be to extend a new line of services to the community, to establish a company of believers in a particular locality, to improve and extend the church's channels of distribution of the Advent message, or any other marketing alternative that would contribute to the overall mission of the church.

Develop a Core Mission/Ministry Strategy

The core strategy is really a statement or set of

statements that outlines just how the organization will tackle the market challenges. Will it go after the whole market or different segments of the market? An effective core strategy will have the following characteristics:[36]

1. It will be *people centered*. The main focus of the strategy is Christ-centered ministry and services that are sensitive to the needs and inner hunger of lost people. It will not simply force a program on the community (internal or external), or just follow organizational agendas. This does not mean that the ministry or program should be an automatic response to the whims and fancies of postmodern men and women, but it certainly means that we must understand the people who comprise our community so well, that we can connect with them in a meaningful way, and capture their interest through our value-based ministries and programs.

2. It will be *visionary*. It will articulate a future for the church that offers a clear sense as to where the church is going, and what will happen when it gets there.

3. It will *differentiate* the church from its key rivals. The church will stand out and offer the target community unique reasons to prefer its ministries and services over those of the competition. Our differentiation should not just be limited to doctrinal truth and the peculiarities of the Adventist lifestyle, but must be extended to, and be confirmed by, our openness and willingness to love people—all kinds of people. The compelling power and magnetism of genuine love and unabridged communal fellowship among us must be the badge of the people of God. "By THIS [our ability

MARKET SENSITIVE MISSION AND MINISTRY

to mirror His love in the community of faith]," said Jesus, "shall everyone [*even the unchurched, the non-Christian, and secular, post-modern people*] know that you are MY DISCIPLES" (John 13:35, emphasis mine). The bottom line is that people will know that we are the remnant people of God not by our doctrines (as important as those are to our denominational identity), but by the reflection of the character of Jesus in a mighty display of healing, converting, and all-embracing love.

4. It will be *sustainable* in the long run, in the face of likely competitors' reactions. Once a strategy is successful, a competitor is most likely to react, and the organization should anticipate this possibility and prepare for it. Love is *always sustainable*. Doctrine, teaching, and lifestyle may be amended from time to time, but "love bears all things, believes all things, hopes for all things, endures all things. Love never fails" (1 Corinthian 13:7, 8).

5. It will be *easily communicated*. The central elements of the strategy will be simple and clear enough so that both the customer and members of the organization will have an unambiguous understanding as to why it should be supported. While a certain amount of capitalization on electronic media for the spreading of the gospel is strategic and necessary, it should not become the dominant strategy since it is not easily duplicable by church communities or individual members. There is an urgent need to return to the simple rudiments of the gospel and primitive discipleship among the people of God, so that the larger share of the body

of believers may be incorporated into the overall strategy for reaching the world for Jesus Christ and the Kingdom of God. This will be dealt with more fully later on.

6. It will be *motivating*. A successful strategy will have the enthusiastic commitment of those who will carry it out. Motivation is increased by participation, evaluation, affirmation, and spiritual renewal. Mission and ministry that place the believing community in a spectatorial role often stifle creativity and destroy motivation.

7. It will be *flexible*. The strategy should be broad enough to allow for a range of application based upon the uniqueness of the individuals using it. It should not be so rigid and uncompromising that it cannot be adaptable to unforeseen situations. After all, one size does not fit all.

In the past, the church has practiced a mass marketing approach to its evangelistic mission. The big tents were for "whosoever would," and many have come. However, though the results were good, they were also skewed along the lines of Christians from other denominations, with very little success among non-Christians and the un-churched. While tent-crusades could be maintained as an ongoing but strategically monitored activity, there is also a very urgent need to explore other methods.

Targeting an audience is an important step in defining the mission of the congregation. It puts a human face on the ministry's purpose.[37] Once a congregation settles on its audience, it can design an approach to these people that may open the door for the entrance of the transforming gospel of

Jesus Christ. Warren writes: "Catching fish on their terms means letting your target determine your approach. When you go fishing, do you use the same kind of bait for every kind of fish? Of course not. Do you use the same size of hook for every kind of fish? No. You must use the bait and hook that best matches the fish you want to catch."[38]

It would be very wise for church leaders to consider segmenting the territory's population to help make the following strategic decisions:[39]

1. Quantity decisions: How much of the church's financial, human and mental resources are to be devoted to each segment?

2. Quality decisions: How would each segment be approached in terms of specific ministries, communications, ministry venue, costs, and the like?

3. Timing decisions: When should a specific ministry be directed at particular segments?

The church may, therefore, choose to segment a particular community possibly along ethnic, geographical, religious and non-religious lines, since one approach would never successfully reach everyone. Further, it may not be at all practical or economically feasible for the church to effectively address all segments at the same time. Wise leadership would therefore consider target ministry or niche ministry, based on the church's resources, quality of its services (ministries) and programs, and timing of mission activity. For example, the church may find that its unique position on health or prophetic interpretation, as well as its community service programs can provide a distinct and advantageous ministry niche over other religious groups in a particular location.

Develop Competitive Position

Once the community segment(s) has been decided upon, the church should adopt a competitive positioning strategy toward its target audience. Kotler and Andreasen define positioning as the "act of designing the organization's image and value offer so that the organization's customers understand and appreciate what the organization stands for in relation to its competitors."[40] This involves creating a real differentiation from other competitors and making it known to everyone.

In many communities around the world our church does not enjoy a healthy public image. Efforts should be made to eradicate these barriers to the church's mission by ascertaining the cause of such biases and by repositioning the church in a more positive light. Positioning strategies must be clearly identifiable by non-members and should project images of the church that offer some value to these non-members. For example, positioning strategies may offer community values such as caring family, loving community, children and youth advancement, hope, open fellowship, biblical teaching, etc.

The basic idea of the positioning strategy is to design an image of the church that resonates with societal values, and also clearly sets that community of faith distinctly apart from others. On this matter, George Barna says, "competitive positioning aids people's recall of your church in a positive, believable, and helpful light."[41] Steve Dunkin made the informative comment that "everything the church does tends to create an image . . . including the architectural style of the building, the way the grounds are kept, the greeters at the door (or lack of them), the type of music, the style of a church sign, and the order of service—to name a few."[42]

We must be prepared to ask ourselves the very hard, but realistic, questions: What does the local community think about us? When the name of our church is mentioned in conversation, what type of reaction does it bring out in people? The results of surveys conducted by the North American Division, in an effort to determine the public's awareness of our church in the areas of (1) name recognition, (2) attitude toward the church, (3) church's image, and (4) mission impact, show that we do have some very serious work to do. In 1970, 65 percent of the public surveyed had heard of the Seventh-day Adventist Church. In 1986 the number increased to 70 percent, but in 1994 it dropped to 53 percent. This means that in 1994 little more than half of the Americans and Canadians surveyed had ever heard of our church.[43] What was even more revealing was the increase in the number of persons who misidentify us with the Church of Jesus Christ of Latter-day Saints (Mormons) or Jehovah's Witnesses. In 1986, this confusion that linked us to those two groups ranked as the seventh most frequent response to the question regarding attitude towards the Adventist Church, but by 1994, this misidentification of our church with Jehovah's Witnesses and the Mormons jumped to the fourth spot.[44]

Surely this major misidentification is the result of a lack of knowledge about Seventh-day Adventism and can only be remedied when the church, as a whole, becomes more intentional and practical in discipling believers to permeate the communities where they live, work, and play, with a positive Christian witness. Besides giving careful consideration to the above-mentioned factors regarding their positioning strategy, church leaders and members could also prayerfully weigh what characteristics of the church or congregation really matter to the target audience—possibly a caring community image, or a community dedicated to truth and quality service, or some other position.

However, nothing is gained by positioning the church in a manner that is irrelevant to its target market.[45] For example, when we position the Seventh-day Adventist Church as "the Remnant Church of Bible Prophecy" (as true as this may be), non-Christians, the unchurched, and even many Protestants haven't the faintest idea of what we are talking about; yet we expect these very people to be drawn by this idea that is so foreign to them, just because being the remnant is important to us. The truth of the matter is that very few people stay around long enough to hear our very lengthy explanation of what we mean by the word "remnant" and how we arrive at our unique conclusion and authoritative claim. Still we continue to use this same positioning strategy, hoping that the rest of the world will share our perception regarding this claim and embrace the teachings of Adventism. While we have no doubt of who we are as a people, we need to seriously consider positioning our church with a people perspective. Instead of gazing at organizational agendas, we should take an honest look at what is going on in our communities and feel the heart-cries of hurting, lonely, frustrated, hopeless, and confused people. This would bring a different perspective to the way we position ourselves to a hurting world. No longer will "who we are" be the dominant factor in the way we portray ourselves, but "what we feel" in common with our society, as we immerse ourselves in ministry to its pain. Interestingly, Steve Dunkin suggests that the church could also choose to position, what he calls, a "faith image." He says that "as men and women of vision, our motto should be . . . Believing is Seeing! In other words, there is no need for you to be bound by the present image of your church, especially if that image is an unfavorable one. Reach out, by faith, become the church that you believe God is calling you to be and intends you to be!"[46]

How important is a positioning strategy? Let me put it this way. Strategic positioning is of such crucial importance that even God found it necessary to position Himself in His Son (the *most powerful expression and demonstration of His love for humanity*), in order to nullify the negative perception of His character that Satan was seeking (and still seeks) to plant into the minds of human beings. Ellen White explains, "the enemy of good blinded the minds of men, so that they looked upon God with fear and thought of Him as severe and unforgiving. Satan led men to conceive of God as a being whose chief attribute is stern justice—one who is a severe judge, a harsh, exacting creditor. He pictured the Creator as a being who is watching with jealous eye to discern the errors and mistakes of men, that He may visit judgments upon them."[47] She also wrote, "Satan is constantly at work, with intense energy and under a thousand disguises, to misrepresent the character and government of God. With extensive, well-organized plans and marvelous power, he is working to hold the inhabitants of the world under his deceptions."[48]

Even though God is all compassionate, loving, kind, forgiving, longsuffering, merciful and just, to name a few divine attributes, it is of pivotal significance to Him that human beings see (though through a glass darkly—1 Corinthians 13) these perceptions of His character, so that He can draw and save them. Thus, He sent His Only Son and our Savior as a full expression and guarantee of His love and as a sign of His complete commitment to save us. The Word of God emphatically declares, *"no one has ever seen God. It is God the only Son, who is close to the Father's heart, who has made him known"* (John 1:18 NRSV). And Jesus (God's positioning strategy) proclaimed: *"I came down from heaven, not to do mine own will, but the will of Him who sent me"* (John 6:38).

Over and over again in the gospels, Jesus made

reference to His unique role as the Father's voice, life, and work here on earth (Matthew 11:27; Luke 10:22; John 5:19, 36-38; 6:44-46; 12:49). So God positioned Himself in His Son so that He could reconcile the world unto Himself (See 2 Corinthians 5:18). As Jesus portrayed (positioned) God to the world, God drew people to Himself. Jesus said: *"No one can come to me unless drawn by the Father who sent me"* (John 6:44; see also verse 65 NRSV).

The sinner's perception of God is vitally important to the plan of salvation and God's redemptive purpose on earth, because sinners would never be drawn to a God they perceive as harsh, un-forgiving, vindictive, vengeful, and unappeasable. As a matter of fact, eternal life hinges upon the sinner's knowledge of God as revealed through His Son (John 17:3). It is a fact that a person's relationship to God is directly related to that person's perception of God. In sending us Jesus, God intended to refute Satan's misrepresentation of His character and to give the whole world a corrective view of who He was, and is, and evermore shall be. Our unique doctrinal positions on human suffering, the state of the dead, hell, and the punishment of the wicked, which stand against Satan's perennial attacks on the character of God, are invaluable contributions to Christendom and the world.

Christ's representation of the Father was so complete that He declared: *"I and my Father are one"* (John 10:30). On one occasion, Philip uttered the heart's cry of earth's searching pilgrims: *"Lord, show us the Father, and we will be satisfied"* (John 14:8 NRSV). In other words, *"Lord, don't just tell us what God is like. We want to see Him for ourselves and we will be satisfied."* Jesus' reply surprised Philip and the other disciples and may still confuse earth's teeming multitudes today. He said: *"Have I been with you all this time, Philip, and you still do not know me? Whoever has seen me has seen the Father. How can you say, 'Show us the Father'? Do you not believe that I am in the Father and the Father is in me? The words that I say to you I do not speak of my own; but the Father who dwells in me does His works. Believe me that I am in the Father and the Father is in me"* (John 14:8-11 NRSV).

As God's positioning strategy, Jesus clearly and unequivocally portrayed the loving and perfect character of the Father to the universe. Through His vicarious death on Calvary, He unmasked Satan's pejorative propaganda against God and convincingly demonstrated the Father's loving concern for His lost children. "Since Jesus came to dwell with us, we know that God is acquainted with our trials, and sympathizes with our griefs. Every son and daughter of Adam may understand that our Creator is the friend of sinners. For in every doctrine of grace, every promise of joy, every deed of love, every divine attraction presented in the Saviour's life on earth, we see 'God with us.'"[49]

On the evening of His resurrection, Jesus' commission to His disciples (and to us) was: "As the Father has sent me, so I send you" (John 20:21 NRSV). Therefore, as Christ's representatives on earth we must be committed to reflecting His character to the world as He reflected the character of His heavenly Father. It is not safe or productive for us to ignore, or dismiss as insignificant, non-members' perceptions of our church. In Jesus' day, the elect people of God ignored the needs, feelings, and perceptions of the Gentiles and were rejected by Jehovah as His appointed agency to bear His message of hope and love to the then-known world. As God's people in these last days, we dare not do the same to the unbelieving world.

Since non-members' perception of Adventism is the only reality they have that will determine their willingness to interact with the church, and thereby get a glimpse of Jehovah, we would be better off by making sure we strategically position the church in the most positive and relevant manner. Thus, the church should be given the opportunity to occupy a special spot in the minds of outside observers, making it easier for them to identify the church from its other competitors and, also, opening the door for them to engage with insiders (believers). The bottom line of all our positioning strategies should be the portrayal of the character of Jesus. Ellen White says, "Christ is sitting for His portrait in every disciple. Every one God has predestinated to be 'conformed to the image of His Son' (Romans 8:29). In every one Christ's longsuffering love, His holiness, meekness, mercy, and truth are to be manifested to the world."[50]

Just as Christ positioned God to the world, we too must position our Savior to this last day generation. Just as Jesus lifted up His Father and God drew men to Himself, we too must lift up Jesus, and He will draw and save all men. He said: *"And I, if I be lifted up from the earth, will draw ALL men unto me"* (John 12:32). Like Philip, the heart's cry of many lost people (and even many professed Christians) is: "Show us this Jesus, whom you say loves me and died for me, and I will believe."

How shall we as a community of faith respond to this all-important request of lost humanity? Is it by flaunting our claims to remnancy, or outlining the irrefutable nature of the cardinal doctrines of our faith? These are very important theological issues, but they must be put in their rightful place in relation to Jesus. May I suggest that the ONLY appropriate response to this request ("Show us this Jesus") is the one Jesus gave: *"Whoever has seen me has seen the Father"* (John 14:8). Can we like Jesus say: "Whoever has seen us has seen the Savior?" If not, why not? Could it be that we are giving preeminence to proving that we are "the remnant" to the world over reflecting who Jesus is? Have we been more preoccupied with positioning the correctness and grandeur of Adventism with little snippets of the Savior, or on reflecting the full character of Jesus to humanity?

If we are to give the most appropriate response to the world's inquiry to see Jesus, we must center the attention and the affections of our people on Him. Everything we do as a religious community must not only be centered on Him, but must also be reflective of Him. We must be more committed to positioning Jesus Christ fully to the world, and "give" Him the freedom to draw whomsoever He wills to Himself.

Notes

1. George Barna, *User Friendly Churches* (Ventura, CA: Regal Books, 1991), 42-43.
2. Walt Kallestad, *Entertainment Evangelism: Taking the Church Public* (Nashville: Abingdon Press, 1996), 103.
3. Barna, *Marketing the Church*, 24.
4. Kotler and Levy, 15
5. Gregory Moorehead and Ricky W. Griffin, *Organizational Behavior* 3rd ed. (Boston: Houghton Mifflin Company, 1992), 363.
6. Douglas Webster, 20.
7. This title represents an adoption of the strategic marketing planning process by Philip Kotler and Alan Andreasen, in *Strategic Marketing for Non-profit Organizations* (Englewood Cliffs, NJ: Prentice Hall, 1991).
8. Migliore and others, *Church and Ministry Strategic Planning: From Concept to Success*, 21-22.
9. Ibid.
10. Kotler and Andreasen, 66-120.
11. Thomas J. Peters and Robert H. Waterman, Jr., "In Search of Excellence," (New York: Harper and Row, 1982), in Philip Kotler and Alan Andreasen, *Strategic Marketing for Nonprofit Organizations* (Englewood Cliffs, New Jersey: Prentice Hall, 1991), 75.
12. Rick Warren, *The Purpose Driven Church: Growth Without Compromising Your Message and Mission* (Grand Rapids: Zondervan Publishing House, 1995), 98.
13. Ibid., 103-106.
14. Kotler and Andreasen, 72.
15. Ibid, 80.
16. The Seventh-day Adventist five-tiered organizational structure is comprised of the local congregation on the lowest level; then the Conference, which is made up of a number of churches in a specific geographical area; then the Union , which consists of a number of local Conferences; next is the Division, which oversees a number of Unions, over a larger geographic area; and then the General Conference, which is the highest governing authority of the Church, and oversees the Divisions.
17. Michael Hammer and James Champy, *Reengineering the Corporation: A Manifesto for Business Revolution* (New York: Harper Business, 1993), 32.
18. Ibid., 33.
19. Ibid.
20. Howard Snyder, *The Problem of Wineskins* (Downers Grove, IL:

InterVarsity Press, 1976), 23-24.
21. George R. Knight, *The Fat Lady and The Kingdom* (Boise, ID: Pacific Press Publishing Association, 1995), 52.
22. Colin Hastings, *The New Organization* (London, England: McGaw-Hill, 1993), 3.
23. C. Peter Wagner, *Churchquake!* (Ventura, CA: Regal Books, 1999), 72.
24. Hammer and Champy, 34.
25. Thomas F. O'Dea, *Sociology and the Study of Religion: Theory, Research, Interpretation* (New York: Baisc Books, Inc., 1970), 240-255.
26. Hammer and Champy, 35.
27. Kallestad, 105-106.
28. George Barna, *The Second Coming of the Church* (Nashville: Word Publishing, 1998), 177.
29. James Emery White, *Rethinking the Church* (Grand Rapids: Baker Book, 1997), 69.
30. Warren, 108.
31. Ibid., 108-109.
32. James Emery White, 71.
33. David A. Aaker and George S. Day, *Marketing Research* (New York: John Wiley & Sons, 1983), 4.
34. Kotler, 130-140.
35. George Barna, *The Frog in the Kettle* (Ventura, CA: Regal Books, 1990), 93.
36. Kotler and Andreasen, 165-166.
37. Wright, 51.
38. Warren, 196-197.
39. See Kotler and Andreasen, *Strategic Marketing for Nonprofit Organizations* for a more comprehensive treatment of market segmentation.
40. Kotler and Andreasen, 205.
41. George Barna, *A Step-by-step Guide to Church Marketing*, (Ventura, CA: Regal Books, 1992), 151.
42. Steve Dunkin, *Church Advertising, A Practical Guide*, (Nashville: Abingdon Press, 1982), 49.
43. See *Public Awareness: The Perceptions and Attitudes of the General Public Towards the Seventh-day Adventist Church*, comps. Paul Richardson et al (Portland, OR: Baby Boomer Ministries Resource Center, 1994), 23-24. This study was commissioned by the Office of Information and Research of the North American Division of Seventh-day Adventists.
44. Ibid.
45. Barna, *A Step-by-step Guide to Church Marketing*, 152.

46. Dunkin, 50.
47. Ellen G. White, *Happiness Digest* (Washington, DC: Better Living Publications, 1983), 2.
48. White, *Patriarchs and Prophets* (Hagerstown, MD: Review And Herald Publishing Association, 1958), 78.
49. White, *Desire of Ages*, 24.
50. Ibid. 827.

7

TOWARDS A MORE STRATEGIC APPROACH

Strategic Mission/Ministry Planning Process – Part II

Design the Mission/Ministry Mix

Once the Church's positioning strategy is carefully defined, it will make transparently clear the principal elements that must be in its marketing (mission and ministry) mix,[1] and will also reflect the need for careful mix coordination. In the context of the church, these elements will comprise the Product, Price, Place of Distribution and Promotion, details of which are provided below:

    1. Product: The Christian "product" (if I am permitted to use such a designation) is essentially the good news of the gospel and the Christian lifestyle called forth by its proclamation. There are also many attributes to this "product." It can be featured in different *sizes* (since one size does not fit all), *forms* (since these tend to change with time), *brands* (since people are culturally and ethnically different), and *packaging* (since people tend to be drawn by what they perceive will satisfy their needs or desires – real or imaginary). However, it is very important to understand that

while the "core product" does not change, the expressions of the product through these external characteristics do change with time.

As Christians, we must develop the art of understanding our target audience so well (through caring friendships), that we can tailor our ministry offerings to fit their needs. Warren says that if we are going to catch fish, we must learn to think like fish.[2] This does not mean that we have to live like them, or even act like them, but it certainly means that we have to understand them. In order to do that, we must mingle with them as Christ did—that is, in ways that make them feel the completeness of our identification with their interests and happiness.[3] To nail down his point, Warren further states, "in order to catch fish, it helps to understand their habit preferences, and feeding patterns. Certain fish like smooth, still water, and others like to swim in rushing rivers. Some fish are bottom crawlers, and others like to hide under the rocks."[4] In other words, unsaved people have different "feeding" patterns because they are driven by a wide variety of different motives. Some of these people are "night-crawlers," others are "day-dreamers," and still others have haunts, habitats, and addictions that are very repulsive. However, our marching orders demand that we find ways to bait and hook these helpless, hopeless feeders in the broken cisterns of this world, for the Kingdom of Heaven.

Let me introduce a word of caution here. Fishing can be a very dangerous enterprise, whether we are doing it from the shore, a rock, on a bridge, or in a boat. We face the constant peril of falling into the water (God help us if we cannot swim), being blown to bits by a storm at sea, or being left to drift in the ocean of nowhere, due to engine failure. Fish can also lure us into some very strange, precipitous places, and we must be ready for the occasion. Working for lost people, who are caught up in all sorts of unimaginable sin and vice that are present in our world today, can be likened to fishing in deep and treacherous waters. Ellen White says, "those who are seeking to rescue others from vice and ruin, are especially exposed to temptation. In constant contact with evil, they need a strong hold upon God lest they themselves be corrupted."[5]

Deep-sea fishing is not for everyone, and should not be attempted by anyone who has not been adequately trained and equipped for this challenge. As Christian fishermen, we must be aware of our mental, physical, and spiritual limitations, and work within the sphere of our God-given abilities and competencies. It is foolhardy to try to fish for people in someone else's gear. Like David before Saul (1 Samuel 17:20-58), we must be willing to lay aside the armor of the "king fishers" (like E. E. Cleveland, C. D. Brooks, Kembleton Wiggins, Walter Pearson, Mark Finley, or Kenneth Cox, to name a few), and go forth (like David) to slay the Goliaths of this evil world in the mighty armor of God.

As we fish for people, it is very important for us to remember that it is "only through a living faith in Christ as personal Savior is it possible to make our influence felt in a skeptical world. If we would draw sinners out of the swiftrunning current, our own feet must be firmly set upon the Rock, Christ Jesus."[6] "We cannot give to others that which we do not ourselves possess."[7]

The Christian product (that is, the Christian lifestyle in terms of faith and practice) is not an easy sell, because it runs across the grain of the thinking of modern society. Even Christ had a very difficult time trying to present the cross (one aspect of the Christian product) to His own disciples (Matt 16:21-26). In speaking about proclaiming the cross in a secular world very much like ours, Paul said: *"For the preaching of the cross is to them that perish foolishness; but unto us which are saved it is the power of God"* (1 Cor 1:18). *"But the natural man receiveth not the things of the Spirit of God: for they are foolishness unto him: neither can he know them, because they are spiritually discerned"* (1 Cor 2:14).

If there was ever a time when these passages of Scripture had great significance for the preaching of the gospel, that time is today. The preaching of the cross, in the context of the gospel, is foolish to this age that exalts human wisdom as the ultimate source of authority. Church leaders are, therefore, challenged to package the gospel in such a way that it would not only be in harmony with the church's positioning strategy, but that its features, styling, and branding would make it identifiable and appealing to the Church's target population.

It would also be very helpful to remember that the Christian offering is two-dimensional and must be presented as such. It portrays not only the word proclaimed, but also the life lived. It is not only theoretical, but also practical and relational. Ellen White wrote: "Not all the books written can serve the purpose of a holy life. Men will believe, not what the minister preaches, but what the Church lives. Too often the influence of the sermon preached from the pulpit is counteracted by the sermon preached in the lives of those who claim to be advocates of truth."[8] She also said, "there is an eloquence far more powerful than the eloquence of words in the quiet, consistent life of a pure, true Christian. What a man is has more influence than what he says."[9]

2. Price: This represents any cost, real or imaginary, that a person perceives he or she has to pay to become a Christian. This cost is often perceived as treasured objects, ideas, and even total lifestyle that must be given up in order to take up the life that Christ offers. It involves an intellectual and emotional commitment to Jesus Christ and His cause. Jesus said: *"If any want to become my followers, let them deny themselves and take up their cross and follow me"* (Matt 16:24 NRSV). There is a real cost to discipleship, and Jesus did not hesitate to make this absolutely clear. The Bible says in Luke 14:25-33:

> Now large crowds were traveling with Him; and he turned and said to them, "Whoever comes to me and does not hate father and mother, wife and children, brothers and sisters, yes, and even life itself, cannot be my disciple. Whoever does not carry the cross and follow me cannot be my disciple. For which

of you, intending to build a tower, does not first sit down and estimate the cost, to see whether he has enough to complete it? Otherwise, when he has laid a foundation and is not able to finish, all who see it will begin to ridicule him, saying, 'This fellow began to build and was not able to finish.' Or what king, going out to wage war against another king, will not sit down first and consider whether he is able with ten thousand to oppose the one who comes against him with twenty thousand? If he cannot, then, while the other is still far away, he sends a delegation and asks for terms of peace. So therefore, none of you can become my disciple if you do not give up all your possessions." (NRSV)

Therefore, the object of the Christian persuader (marketer), in this context is not to reduce the cost of discipleship, but to make sure that the quality and value of what Jesus offers exceeds, by far, the disciple's cost. In other words, the followers of Christ must be able to show by proclamation and practice that the quality and fullness of life that Christ offers in the here and now, and the eternal rewards of life everlasting, extend the best benefits to the potential disciple when compared with any alternative lifestyle.

3. <u>Place of Distribution</u>: This has to do with the movement of the Christian product, in terms of message and life, from the church to the community. This is a very important aspect of the ministry mix and would therefore

require a more thorough treatment than the other elements in the mix. Without an effective system of distribution, it would be rather difficult for any organization to get products and services to the marketplace in order to earn a fair profit. If the church is to be successful in winning the world for Christ, it must endeavor to develop multiple channels of distribution through which it seeks to disseminate the good news of the gospel.

There is definitely room for enlarging upon, re-defining (in terms of mission objective and changing public needs), and possibly re-positioning current distribution channels available to the church. These channels include and are not limited to the churches, schools, Adventist Book Centers, radio and television stations, World Wide Web, colporteurs, Adventist literature, crusades, cottage meetings, Bible studies, and other church-related activities. Moreover, church members must be aware that channels of distribution exist wherever they live, and work, and play; and these should be explored for opportunities to share their faith and witness. There is also the urgent need in some quarters for our members to move away from the attitude that says: "We have the truth, so come and get it."

Distribution opportunities exist wherever people exist. Therefore, we need to deploy our distribution forces and resources wherever the people are. Community-based projects and information and distribution centers (health, welfare, etc.) that address quality-of-life issues are valuable, but under-utilized, avenues that can help the church connect with society. The 1994 Public Awareness Research, commissioned by the Office of Information and Research of the North American Division (NAD), indicates that of the 53 percent of the population who are aware of our existence, a staggering 82 percent of them say they have no idea about Adventist community involvement, and only 15 percent agree that we are supportive of preserving the environment.[10]

We need to tap into these fertile arenas and make a positive impact for the cause of Christ. Warren makes a very valid point that "churches that expect the unchurched to show up simply because they build a building and hang out a 'We're Open' sign are deluding themselves. People don't voluntarily jump into your boat. You must penetrate their culture. To penetrate their culture you must be willing to make some concessions in matters of style in order to gain a hearing."[11]

In order to accomplish this penetration, we need to engage with the unchurched on their "turf," seeking to understand them, their needs, their dreams and aspirations, and their motive force. Like the salt of the earth, we need to mingle with a motive—that is, to position the positive, converting influence of a consistent Christian life in order to lead the unchurched to Christ. Mission and ministry channels exist wherever the believer happens to be, at any time of day or night, and we must keep this mission perspective continually and consistently before the people of God.

Dan Day says, "we market best when we do it right where we are, in our circle of friends, business associates, and fellow-travelers. And we do it by being *real* for Christ, allowing Him to impress us with His commitment to people and use us to meet their needs."[12] In this context, he suggests that "the key to a vigorous witness [good marketing] is for us as Christians to begin expanding our circle of involvement, so that our influence can be felt in the widest possible scope – on the job, on the Little League field, at school, at the social services center, at the lake, and behind the wheel."[13] In support of this approach, Bill Hull emphatically states: "There is no impact without contact. Unless we go where the fish are, we won't catch any. The Pharisees weren't catching anyone; they were fishing in a stained-glass aquarium and were coming up empty. The reason the Church has been so inept in evangelism is partly due to the pharisaic unwillingness to live in *the real world*"[14] (italics mine).

In a more specific sense, Warren suggests that we are to go where the fish are biting.[15] He says "it is a waste of time to fish in a spot where the fish aren't biting. Wise fishermen move on. They understand that fish feed in different spots at different times of the day. Nor are they hungry all the time."[16] He based this cogent observation on reality fishing and the principle of receptivity, as depicted in Jesus' parable on the "Sower and the Soils" (Matthew 13:3-23). The harvest principle suggests that we pick the fruits that are ripe first, but not to the neglect of those that are green. As workers together with God, we can help create conditions that could transform green fruits into ripe ones, ready for the picking.

Going where the fish are has been a major challenge

for us as a church, since we have traditionally done evangelism from what is referred to as the "fortress model." We live in isolated, protective, and cliquish societies, and sally out only to capture a few souls from our barbarous surroundings. Once captured, we pull these sultry souls into our fort, and raise the drawbridge over the "moat" that separates us from the rest of the world. Instinctively, we begin the work of spiritual nurture and conservation, which often involves further indoctrination and denominational inoculation.

Very often in our conservation process, we groom new believers by promptly alienating them from family, friends, former church family, and the world. By making use of a misapplication of Paul's admonition to "come out from among them and be ye separate,"[17] new believers are taught to distance themselves from practically all their former associations in order to protect their newly found faith. Most of them follow through on this call to separation in order to be accepted into the Adventist culture and community as a member in good and regular standing.

Myron Widmer insightfully observed that as a Christian community, "we have done a great job of providing spiritual nurturing environments at our churches, and of providing Adventist alternatives for almost everything in society—alternatives that keep most of us from interfacing and working with (and getting contaminated by?) other community residents. We have our own churches, schools, Pathfinder Clubs, socials, summer camps, retirement centers, hospitals, sports teams, professional business associations, and mission endeavors. You name it, and we've created our own version of it."[18]

Nothing is wrong with these amenities in and of themselves, except when we allow them to undermine or inhibit our ability to meaningfully engage the world for Christ. I am afraid that many of our people have grown so accustomed to our Adventist brands of the world's goods and services that they sense little need for any friendly contact with the real world, except when some type of evangelistic campaign necessitates them doing so. It is no wonder, therefore, why many of our people have so much difficulty sharing their faith with people of the world: it is because they have very few friends in the world and are not adept at making friends for fear of losing faith in the process. In the 1994 Public Awareness Survey commissioned by the NAD, less than a quarter of the group who were aware of the existence of Seventh-day Adventists (that is, 53% of the interviewees) knew an Adventist personally on the job or in the neighborhood. More than three-quarters (79%) of the aware group had never even visited a Seventh-day Adventist Church. How can we ever hope to impact our non-Adventist communities without any meaningful contact with the people who live in them?

If we will make our influence felt in this skeptical world, we cannot practice conservation by isolation. Instead we must follow Jesus' approach of conservation by infiltration. We must consistently employ the "*go-home-to-your-friends-and-tell-them*" principle (Mark 5:19) established by the Master Teacher Himself. Jesus also said: *"For whoever wishes to save his life shall lose it; but whoever loses his life for My sake shall find it"* (Matthew 16:25 NASV). Self-preservation is a very strong motivator of human behavior, and when that trait becomes institutionalized it can eclipse organizational vision and creativity and inhibit the organization's ability and willingness to act. The organization becomes very risk-averse and reactive (instead of pro-active) because people within it are paralyzed by fear of the unknown. The resulting mode of organizational operations tends to protect and preserve, rather than explore and expend.

As a community of faith, we must make every effort to ensure that our discipleship practices do not isolate converts from the communities from which they were extracted, but should incorporate instructing and training them to connect with their former friends without disconnecting their faith. Deploy these new believers to infiltrate their neighborhoods with the good news of God's saving grace on their lips. Allow them to experience the operation of God's power in their lives and testimonies. The tendency to concentrate our effort on trying to make new believers loyal Adventists, rather than fruit-bearing disciples at the onset of their new experience in Christ, limits their ability to make an impact for the Kingdom among their friends and neighbors.

However, the biblical model given by the Master Teacher calls for the reverse to this very principle. The gospel commission calls us, first and foremost, to *make disciples* of new believers, and, in the process, we are to teach them to observe all things (Matthew 28:19, 20). While church membership has become the accepted norm (since the Protestant Reformation) for bringing new believers to the body of Christ, we must remember that it is not our Biblical mandate. The command of Christ is exceptionally clear. We have been commissioned to make disciples, and to teach disciples to make more disciples, not just members of some particular denomination or organization (be they Seventh-day Adventist or otherwise).

Sadly, our evangelistic process has been tailored more toward making non-Adventists (churched and unchurched) members of the remnant church than disciples of Jesus Christ, and, most frequently, the process of evangelization stops once these new believer are baptized and received into the church. Even in our conservation process we focus our attention and resources more on membership issues than on discipleship issues, on denominational issues more than Kingdom issues, on the remnant Church more than on the returning Christ. What we have as a result is a large number believers who are very loyal to the church and its teaching, but not so to their Master and His mandate because of the Master's call to discipleship was never made the hallmark and motto of their religious experience.

The Master's methods alone will give evangelistic success to the mission of the Seventh-day Adventist Church. However, we must return to the divine blue print of making and training disciples for the Kingdom of God, and to laying on them the full costs[19] of Christ's invitation: "Follow Me!" What was Christ's plan for growing His Kingdom? He simply made disciples and immediately trained them to make more disciples. At the moment of their conversion and surrender to His Lordship, Jesus consistently deployed new converts, as disciples, in the communities where they lived.[20] These disciples of Jesus received on-the-job training, and Christ trusted in the power of God, and their newly found relationship with Him to keep and sustain them. Christ's goal was to make every new believer a disciple (not so much a member) from the onset, and that was, and still is, a very successful strategy.

In an effort to facilitate this success strategy, I would like to introduce the concept of Network Discipling.[21] This involves the training and developing of disciples in an exponential manner. For the sake of space and time, I have chosen to give a brief illustration of this phenomenal concept in the Appendix to this book. However, suffice it to say that this approach will create a multiplicity of distribution points for the dissemination of the gospel of Jesus Christ.

This simple design involves training one disciple to disciple three people, who will, in turn, train each of these three to disciple three more. By this very uncomplicated process of disciple duplication, the body of Christ has the potential to experience super-abounding growth. Bill Hull has rightly said, "the greatest threat to Satan's kingdom is not the American megachurch. It is whenever and wherever a motivated disciple-making pastor coaches an awakened laity to work together. When they do, multiplication is near. To Satan the most frightening thought is that pastors and leaders would take seriously the command of making disciples and multiplying themselves. The exponential growth of the church, through its members, is the most dynamic force possible to man."[22]

4. <u>Promotion</u>: This consists of a variety of techniques, including advertising, sales promotion, public relations, and personal selling, that are used to communicate with customers and potential customers.[23] Christian media is an open, untapped field for the Seventh-day Adventist Church. We are often too reluctant to expose ourselves and our offerings through the various electronic, or literary media available to us today.

I am really impressed by the positive advertisements aired on public television by the Church of Jesus Christ of Latter Day Saints. Despite what we think or know about this religious group, they are reaching out to society with a very positive and powerful positioning strategy. They project themselves, through their advertisements, as a very caring Christian community that delights in growing and nurturing healthy, happy families. Another good example is the YMCA of Frederick, Maryland, USA. Their positive televised message states: "We build strong kids, strong families, strong communities."

In the area of advertising, the church can possibly expand and refine its use of radio, television, and the World Wide Web. We can tap into the business expertise of our own members to design web pages that position the church, its service, and value offerings in a very positive light. We can also redesign our current Adventist literature arsenal so that, in language and format, it may easily cross cultural and sub-cultural boundaries. Moreover, our advertising must take us where the fish are. In the shopping malls, on aircrafts, and in all other busy thoroughfares of life, Adventist literature of all kinds should add their presence and silent witness to the many voices that are clamoring for the attention, time and interest of the masses.

Another area through which the church can make a positive impact on society is that of public relations. There is a need for us to shake off some of our Christian otherness and become more actively involved with the community, by either sponsoring community based programs ourselves, or linking up with other organizations and churches that do. Frequent press releases about in-house events and programs that can benefit the community, as a whole, should become a norm among our churches. We should not rely simply on traditional methods, using language that is filled with in-house clichés to communicate our offerings to the community. Warren says, "If you look at most church advertising, it's obvious that it was written from a believer's viewpoint, not from the mind-set of an unchurched person. . . . No matter how life-changing our message is, it won't do any good if we're broadcasting it on a different channel from the unchurched."[24]

To be effective communicators of the gospel, we must

endeavor to use forms (visual or verbal) of communication that connect with the target population. To cling to archaic traditional forms that have lost their meaning to modern society is to risk being ineffective, misunderstood, and disconnected from the very ones we are trying to reach for Christ.

We must also be willing to deal with the concerns of post-modern society, and show how Christ and the Christian lifestyle relate to them. In this regard, we must seek to utilize forms of communication that are familiar to the target population. This was the approach that Jesus used to reach His audience; "He found access to the minds of His hearers by the pathway of their familiar associations. He had likened the Spirit's influence as the cool, refreshing water. He had represented Himself as the light, the source of life and gladness to nature and to man."[25] Jesus knew how to connect with his audience, and so must we.

Permit me to mention at this point that I am truly impressed with the Oprah Winfrey talk show, which, because of this very principle, has become a household attraction in North America. Oprah has found a way to connect with the American society by using professional expertise and real-life subjects to address the social and personal concerns of the American masses. She and her supporting crew seem to have a very clear objective: to genuinely help people where they are hurting. While it is true that people need Jesus in their lives, it is also true that there are many people (including Christians) who need serious help to cope with living in the real world.

When I think of all the professional expertise that Christ has gathered into our community of faith—counselors, therapists, family life and healthful living educators, teachers, youth leaders, nurses, doctors of all kinds, to name a few—we can run our own talk/action show (form) to connect with society in a real and living way. We can, by this means, open up avenues for the Holy Spirit to really bless the lives of sick, hurting, and confused people. We must use our ingenuity to create points of contact with modern society and give the Holy Spirit multiple options with which to work.

However, there are two major challenges facing the church with regard to choosing appropriate forms for distributing the gospel in the context of Adventism:

(1) The challenge of relating to leaders and believers who equate form with function and, as such, hold some forms more sacred than others. Functions are biblical mandates enjoined on the church for the building and edifying of the body of Christ, and the carrying forth of its mission in the world—for example, evangelism, worship, prayer, fellowship, discipleship, baptism, teaching/preaching, etc. These functions are timeless and should not be altered except to reword and rephrase them for the purpose of communication and remaining culturally relevant.[26] Forms, on the other hand, are timely and culturally based and are subject to alteration if the cultural or social context requires it. For a very long time, the cultural forms of European churches have exerted a major influence on many traditional

North American churches, and can be readily attested to in the liturgical worship, hymn singing, and to a lesser degree, dress.[27] Many of these European forms have lengthy traditions and are regarded as holy untouchables in many traditional churches.

(2) The challenge of dealing with leaders and believers who reject a form of expression, or communication, because it did not originate within the confines of the church. Many times the confusion lies in the inability of some Christians (including Seventh-day Adventists) to separate the form (which in many cases is morally neutral) from the unholy use made of the form. Let me illustrate: The steel pan (or steel drum) is used in the Caribbean islands as the instrument of choice to provide music for revelers during their yearly carnival parades. At one time the steel pan was regarded as a tool of the devil, and was not accepted by our church as a worthy instrument to be played in the house of God. Today, many sit in amazement when they hear the melodious and soul-stirring music that resonates from these steel containers that were originally manufactured to store or ship crude oil.

Jesus counsels us to be "wise as serpents and harmless as doves" (Matthew 10:16). He also said, *"the sons of this age are more shrewd in relation to their own kind than the sons of light"* (Luke 16:8, NASB). There is much we can learn from the children of the world, for they have the uncanny ability to use the forms that connect with today's generation in order to disseminate, in abundance, their ungodly goods and services to a soon-to-perish world. Instead, what do we often do? We sit back in wonder and amazement at the grip Satan has on the world, or become embroiled in criticism of the people whom the devil uses to creatively distribute his merchandise.

Not very long ago, a couple of evangelical ministers made the strategic move to disseminate the gospel of Christ's soon return by using a form that connected with our secular society. Among their many objectives was to infiltrate the culture of Hollywood and make a mark for Jesus Christ. They published a novel called *Left Behind* that sold millions of copies, and became a best seller for the year 2000. Shortly thereafter, they produced a movie based on that novel and invaded Hollywood, cinemas, and theaters across the country with the message of Christ's second coming. Granted, the movie was a misrepresentation of facts regarding the return of Jesus and the true fate of those left behind; but the producers of the movie did find a way (a connecting form) to engage the unchurched, and the post-modern, secular society on their own turf, and challenge their thinking with the reality of the parousia. Needless to say, many of these unsaved people who, otherwise, would have ignored or repulsed the traditional confrontational approach of preaching the gospel, left the movie houses giving some serious consideration to making Jesus Christ a meaningful factor in their lives. *Left Behind* may have well been the bridge for some lost souls to begin their search for the Jesus of the Bible.

While many of our pastors and people remain hung up on the misleading message of the *Left Behind* adventures,

TOWARDS A MORE STRATEGIC APPROACH

I must truly compliment Tim LaHaye and Jerry Jenkins for their most brilliant effort in repackaging their understanding of the parousia and infiltrating the world of the unsaved with a word for Jesus. I do realize that as a believing community we have an obligation to proclaim the truth about Christ's return and the fate of those who are left behind, but we need not come across as critics sitting in ivory towers and behind stained glass windows, while others venture out into the real world and try to engage the lost with the gospel of Jesus Christ.

Immediately following (in some cases before) the airing of the movie, many of our preachers got on the wagon trail with our own views on *Left Behind*. On 3ABN, and in different pulpits throughout the Adventist world, our preachers were serving up Adventist caveats such as "What Left Behind Left Behind," "The Truth About Left Behind," "What Left Behind Left," and so on. Yet, how ironic it is that we were "left behind" in finding a way to connect with secular America and scoring a victory for Christ! I often wonder what would have been our response if LaHaye and Jenkins had presented the unadulterated truth about the second coming of Jesus. However, the *Left Behind* drama should serve as a lesson for us who profess to have the truth for these last days.

At least one thing is certain—that is, the Holy Spirit is not limited by human conventions or criteria in His methods and approaches to save souls from a burning hell. Fishing in the breeding ground of Hollywood is certainly not off limits for the Holy Ghost; He will fish of sinners wherever He can find them. Mel Gibson's movie, "The Passion" was another clear example of God using the silver screen of Hollywood and televisions sets in millions of homes throughout North America (and later around the world) to view the suffering Savior, dying for the sins of the world. This vivid portrayal of Christ's passion broke the sin-ridden hearts of countless sinners filled the movie theaters with dumb-struck and sobbing patrons. Only heaven knows the full impact and outcome of this most remarkable event.

If we do not tax our resources and nurture the environment that allows for creativity and freedom to explore alternative ways to connect with society for the advancement of the gospel, then we will be setting the stage for others to precede us in doing so. The Holy Spirit is not through with Hollywood nor the rest of the world, but is eagerly looking for more Mel Gibsons, Jeremiahs (acting prophets), and all who are to do and dare for the Kingdom of God.

In this very late hour of Earth's history, we should not be too reticent about stepping out of our comfort zone, or out of the common course of things, to create new avenues to reach the soon-to-perish world for Christ. We should not try to bind the Word of God by human tradition or play-it-safe methods, but we must boldly go where we have not gone before and score compelling victories for the cause of Christ. We have the truth, and there is no doubt about that. Let us therefore find ways to arrest the attention of this confused postmodern society and deliver the goods.

Develop Structure, Tactics, and Benchmarks

At this stage, church leaders can set up the organizational structure and management systems for implementing the mission or ministry strategy. Here is a word of caution: It is very easy, and I daresay quite tempting, to utilize existing church structures—board, departments, councils, etc.—to implement the newly formulated mission/ministry strategy, in the hope of saving time and money. Quite to the contrary, if the structure does not fit the strategy, who can calculate the amount of time, energy, and finance that would be consumed in trying to meet the ministry objectives? This is tantamount to having the wrong tools for a very important job. However, this is very much the state of affairs in most organization- centered churches, ours included. Instead of allowing the mission/ministry strategy to determine the size and shape of the organizational structure, these churches continue to use existing structures (some of which are obsolete, unproductive, and financially burdensome) and squeeze the strategy through them. The end result is another organizational program chasing the shadows of intended strategic objectives and goals.

It is recommended that at this very crucial stage in the strategic mission/ministry process, the church be careful and painstaking in evaluating its resources and make the quality decision of matching them with ministry needs. In many of our congregations (and this is being very modest), we face the perennial problem of just filling office slots to run the programs of the church, instead of guiding people to function in the areas of their expertise and giftedness. This approach is less than strategic and undermines the church's ability to deliver the best quality programs and services to its members and the outside community. A major hallmark of most successful corporations in the business world is a strategy called TQM (Total Quality Management). This phenomenon involves the careful management and evaluation of quality in every operational process in the organization for continuous improvement in organizational effectiveness.

In the business of the King of kings, we must do no less. We cannot afford to be shoddy, sloppy, and slothful, or adopt a business-as-usual attitude. Paul tells us in Colossians 3:23, NASB: "Whatever you do, do your work heartily[28] as for the Lord rather than for men, knowing that from the Lord you will receive the reward of the inheritance. It is the Lord Christ whom you serve." For us, TQM means Total Quality Mission/Ministry—a commitment to operational and service quality (from start to finish) in the name of Christ, for His church, and to the world. Kallestad and Schey state, "the processes of Total Quality Ministry consider the continuous improvement in the way congregations do their ministry. This excellence and quality in ministry leads to repeat customers and creates a climate and environment for the work of the Holy Spirit in the lives of people."[29]

Thus, in the carrying forward of the mission/ministry strategy we should endeavor to have TQM in the development of the structures and processes, and in the recruiting, equipping, and motivating of volunteers to manage the same. TQM would require the outlining of detailed tactics for carrying out specific tasks demanded by the strategy, and the setting up of benchmarks to measure interim and final achievement goals of the program. Benchmarking is the art of finding out how and why some churches (regardless of denomination) can perform mission/ministry tasks better than others, with the aim of imitating or improving upon the best practices of those churches.[30] The process involves the following steps:

(1) determine which mission/ministry function to benchmark.

(2) identify the key performance variables to measure, especially those that contribute to corporate community, dynamic discipleship, and non-member satisfaction and transformation.

(3) identify the best-in-class churches for key performance variables.

(4) measure performance of best-in-class churches to see if they are really doing what they and others claim that they are doing.

(5) measure your own church's current performance.

(6) specify programs and actions to close the gap between your church and the best-in-class churches.

(7) implement, and monitor the results.[31]

While benchmarking has the advantages of improving overall organizational quality and reducing myopic visioning,[32] it could also reduce organizational creativity wherever management consistently uses only the performance of other churches as the starting point to accomplish total quality mission/ministry. The goal here is for balance and careful contextualization of all external processes that are incorporated into the life and function of the local church.

Implementation and Reassessment

The planned mission/ministry strategy should be put into action in the targeted area, and its outcome should be carefully measured to see if the set mission, objectives, and goals were effectively met. Hull asks and answers his own question as regards measuring a church's mission success. "How can we measure the effectiveness of the church? By the ability of its members to penetrate *their world* for Christ. The best way and the right way to grow a church is to improve the members' penetration ability."[33] If the mission/ministry objectives and goals were not achieved, then there may be need for adjustment in the core strategy or tactical details, or even both.

The greatest good that can be done for the Seventh-day Adventist Church in all the world is to release the potential of the entire body of believers in creative ministry within and without the worshiping community. While the traditional approaches to ministry may maintain their place as a vital link to our past history, church leaders and members must come to grips with the "hard-to-ignore" challenges facing the church in these times. If the church is to fulfill her mission in this end-time, she must be willing to relate and speak in relevant terms to the contemporary issues facing modern man. Tom Peters[34] suggests that flexibility and adapting to the fast-changing nature of consumer needs is the order of the day, and that the business or church that protects the basic beliefs, but allows members to cut a wide swath, will find greater progress, faster growth, and more creativity.

It is becoming increasingly important for church leaders to see that the motivating and equipping and the witness of church members can no longer be limited to the traditional methods, and the doctrinal approaches of cottage meetings, Bible lessons, lay crusades, or the big tent. All these are good, but besides being worn to the bone, they attract mainly a certain class of people, to the exclusion of others— failing to utilize the full potential of the people of God. Alternate approaches must be sought and new strategies implemented that will open up new ways to reach all classes within the church, and also in the outside world.

Lindgren and Shawchuck said, "the church must intentionally seek to provide many contexts in which sensitive, seeking persons may experience God's presence, gain increased understanding of God's nature and become deeply committed to doing his will."[35] Ellen G. White predicted, "means will be devised to reach hearts. Some of the methods used in this work will be different from the methods used in the work in the past; but let no one, because of this, block the way by criticism."[36] "Let us not forget that different methods are to be employed to save different ones."³⁷

Maybe the time has come for these new and different methods and approaches to be integrated into the total milieu and operations of the Seventh-day Adventist Church. It is the opinion of this writer that adopting the principles of marketing management to serve as tools in motivating and equipping the entire body of Christ in mission and ministry is one of the most viable options available to the church today.

Notes

1. Marketing mix is the four key elements of the marketing strategy– viz. product, promotion, distribution, and price. Bovée and Thill, *Marketing*, 20.
2. Warren, 188.
3. Ellen White, *Gospel Workers* (Washington D.C.: Review and Herald Publishing Association, 1948), 45.
4. Warren, 188.
5. Ellen White, *Ministry of Healing*, 510.
6. Ellen White, *Counsels On Sabbath School Work*, (Washington, D.C.: Review and Herald Publishing Association, 1938), 100.
7. Ellen White, *Thoughts From the Mount of Blessing*, (Mountain View, CA: Pacific Press Publishing Association, 1956), 37.
8. White, *Testimonies for the Church*, vol. 9, 21.
9. Ellen White, *Ministry of Healing* (Mountain View, CA: Pacific Press Publishing Association, 1905), 469.
10. See *Public Awareness: The Perceptions and Attitudes of the General Public toward the Seventh-day Adventist Church*, 14-15.
11. Warren, 196.
12. Day, 174.
13. Ibid., 143.
14. Hull, 102.
15. Warren, 187.
16. Ibid.
17. While Paul's admonition (2 Cor. 6:17) called for complete

separation from the idolatrous, immoral practices at home in the church at Corinth, it is not a justification for the creation of isolated communities of faith, in which believers experience alienation and sometimes develop 'religious hostility' towards people with whom they were formerly associated.

18. Myron Widmer, "Out of the Salt Piles," *Adventist Review* (September, 1996): 5
19. Luke 9:23-25; 14:25-33.
20. See Matthew 4:19 - Jesus' first call to His disciples was "follow me, and I will make you fishers of men." John 4 - the woman at Jacob's well. Mark 5 - the Gerasene demoniac.
21. Refer to Appendix for an overview of this idea through the Network Discipleship Ministry.
22. Bill Hull, *The DiscipleMaking Pastor*, 102.
23. Bovée and Thill, 23.
24. Ibid., 189.
25. White, *Desire of Ages*, 476.
26. See Aubrey Malphurs's Theology of Change, found in *Advanced Strategic Planning* (Grand Rapids: Baker Books, 1999), 54-57.
27. Ibid.
28. The Gk. ek psuch_ literally means *from the soul or bowels of your being.*
29. Walt Kallestad and Steve Schey, *Total Quality Ministry* (Minneapolis: Ausgburg Fortress, 1994), 12.
30. Adopted from Philip Kotler, *Marketing Management*, 234.
31. Ibid, 235.
32. Myopic visioning involves the predisposition of management to look only inside the organization when it is trying to improve its performance. This is usually the case when the leadership within the organization hold to the idea that their way of doing business is the best.
33. Bill Hull, *The DiscipleMaking Pastor*, 113.
34. Tom Peters, "A Passion for Excellence," quoted in Bill Hull, *The Disciple Making Pastor* (Grand Rapids: Fleming H. Revell, 1994), 100.
35. Alvin Lindgren and Norman Shawchuck, *Let My People Go - Empowering Laity for Ministry* (Schaumburg, IL: Organization Resources Press, 1988), 27.
36. Ellen G. White, *Review and Herald.* (September 30, 1902), quoted in *Evangelism* (Washington D.C.: Review and Herald Publishing Association, 1970), 105.
37. White, *Evangelism*, 106.

8

MISSION BEYOND ADVENTISM

Mission in Tension

Despite the successes that have attended the work of the Seventh-day Adventist Church around the world there are some reasons for concern about the way we approach the task of God's mission. The gospel commission of Matthew 28:19, 20 requires that the good news of the kingdom be carried to every nation, tribe, ethnic community and people group in the world. However, the reality is that most of our resources and efforts have targeted mainly one particular sector of the world community—i.e. those who are already professing Christianity. In some cases, we have broken new ground in un-entered territories through the efforts of Adventist Frontier Missions and our Global Mission strategy; but our evangelistic outreach arsenal has been predominantly directed at "apostate Protestantism," to the neglect of secular people, the unchurched, and non-Christian communities.

This trend has been one of the major fallouts of our self-understanding as the "remnant church" of Bible prophecy. Our attention has been so focused on mystical "Babylon" and her daughters, that we do not engage, in any meaningful way, the rest of the world who have little knowledge and serious misconceptions concerning the God of the universe. Thus, we concentrate our efforts on a presentation of the gospel in the context of the Third Angel's Message and the doctrines of Adventism, in order to set the church apart and distinct from its "Babylonian" counterparts. While this approach has been effective in drawing other Christians into the fellowship of Adventist churches around the world, the results have been far from successful among people of non-Christian religions, and secular, unchurched people. Bert B. Beach explains that "Adventists have been most successful in reaching religious or semi-religious people, especially those who are already Christians or influenced by Christianity. They have much greater difficulty in reaching secular people or those of other faiths."[1]

Admittedly, however, our mission strategy has not been user-friendly to secular, postmodern people, since they are not Biblically literate and are essentially ignorant of basic Christianity. These people have great difficulty understanding the simple rudiments of the gospel and often find the language and mode of communication associated with the Adventist message very confusing. The truth of the matter is that even among Protestants (and to a lesser degree in some Adventist circles), people are challenged mentally by the complexity of our message. How, then, can we expect secular, postmodern people to understand our approach to the gospel? The challenge facing those of us who constitute God's remnant people in these last days is not only to call

God's people (other Christians) out of Babylon (apostate Protestantism), but also to call sinners of all worldly persuasions to repentance and salvation in Jesus Christ.

Mission for the Seventh-day Adventist Church cannot be an "either-or" proposition. We cannot resign ourselves, as we have historically done, to tailoring our evangelism to God's people in Babylon, and leaving the conversion of the unsaved world to other Protestants. At this late hour, we must now realign our resources and employ new and different strategies to engage the unsaved masses in our society with the *simple, saving gospel of Jesus Christ*. Our mission, therefore, must be characterized as a dynamic tension that addresses God's people in Babylon, on the one hand, and offers hope and a way of salvation to non-Christians and a secular, postmodern world on the other hand. There is no doubt that we are very much adept in dealing with the former. Our challenge is to make organizational changes that will facilitate the creation of alternative approaches to successfully accomplish the latter.

Christ, ALL And IN ALL

At the very heart of God's mission to save the world looms the impressive figure of the Lamb of God and Savior of the human race, Jesus Christ. The apostle Paul says that *"**it pleased the Father** that in him [Jesus Christ] should **All** fullness dwell; And, having made peace through the blood of his cross, by him [Jesus Christ] to reconcile **All** things in* *earth, or things in heaven. Where there is neither Greek nor Jew, circumcision nor uncircumcision, Babarian, Scythian, bond nor free: but Christ is **All**, and in **All**"* (Colossians 1:19-20, and 3:11emphasis mine).

Christ and His cross are not only the vital link between earth and eternity, but also the rallying point of the plan of salvation, and God's ultimate positioning strategy to draw all sinners to Himself.[2] Thus, the heart and soul of all mission practice should be the elevation and exaltation of Jesus Christ – as Savior, as Sacrifice, as Spokesman (Intercessor), and as Soon-coming King. Ellen White reminds us, "it is by contemplating Christ, by exercising faith in Him, by experiencing for ourselves His saving grace, that we are qualified to present Him to the world. If we have learned of Him, *Jesus will be our theme; His love, burning upon the altar of our hearts, will reach the hearts of the people. The truth will be presented, not as a cold, lifeless theory, but in the **demonstration of the Spirit**"*[3] (emphasis mine).

Could it be that, in the context of Adventism, God's mission has been inundated far more by who we are as a people and denomination, than by who Jesus is as the Savior of the world? Could it be that people see and hear far more about Adventism and far too little about the Jesus at the center of Adventism? Is it possible that we can become so preoccupied with proving that we are the remnant people of God, that we miss God's burden to prove His love for all sinners through the life, death, resurrection, and intercession of our Lord and Savior, Jesus Christ? George Knight explains, "it is all too easy to be an Adventist without being a Christian. In our evangelism and in Adventism's entire outreach program the centrality of Christ needs to be made crystal clear. The challenge is to consciously structure our outreach so that people become Christians as they become Adventists, since Adventism is meaningless outside of its Christian framework."[4]

If we take an honest look at the way we do evangelism, and candidly ask ourselves the very important question, "What appears to be the central theme, or burden of proof that we present to the dying world?" I believe the honest answer might very well be: "The Seventh-day Adventist Church is the remnant church of Bible Prophecy." Our evangelistic style has always favored spending the largest share of crusade time chalking up arguments to prove that the Seventh-day Adventist Church is what it claims to be. This approach tends to feed our denominational pride as it makes us appear better than the rest of Christendom. However, is proving our remnancy what our mission is all about? Did God call this church for it to prove to the world that He called it, or did He call it to lovingly portray His character to the world and to prepare a people for soon return of Jesus? I am afraid that sometimes we allow our denominational pride to get in the way of the mission that God has really called us to perform.

We must be very careful that we do not allow the *who* of our mission to overshadow, in any way, the *why* and *what* of our mission. The *who* focuses on our calling as God's chosen agency to proclaim His last message of mercy to a dying world. The *why* and *what* have to do with God's reason for calling us and His expectations of us with regard to the salvation of lost men and women. Quite often, we spend so much time emphasizing the *who* of our mission that it becomes an obstacle in the way for us to achieve the *what* of our mission.

We try very hard to prove that the Seventh-day Adventist Church is where God's action is, but what do the non-Adventists and secular people see and hear? They see and hear, *"You can only be saved by becoming a member of the Seventh-day Adventist Church* (not by receiving Jesus as your Savior from sin)." Some might even remark: "You have gone out of your way to prove that you are the remnant church of Bible prophecy, *so what*? What does that have to do with anything?" Moreover, "What does that have to do with me? How does that help me with my addictions or my personal struggles? How can that bring joy and peace to my life? What does that have to do with the Jesus that you folk talk about? That does not say anything about what He could do for me." The list can go on and on. The point is that our approach to secular people does not answer their search for relevance and meaning in this present life.

The perception of our motive, in the minds of the people we are trying to reach for Jesus, is extremely important. Secular, post-modern people may perceive us only as just another denomination trying to make self-righteous, exclusive claims in order to beat the competition.

While intellectual argumentation has its place in some arenas, this approach does not really connect with secular people who are honestly searching for a genuine religious experience. Secular, unchurched people are more or less tired of being bombarded with the theory of religion and the cerebral exercise of denominational argumentation. Intellectual arguments and theological abstractions are often quite confusing and mentally draining for unchurched, secular people, and they tend to generate an unending list of questions.

What really matters to secular, unchurched people is not theological beliefs (even though these are very important), but the ontological experience of the religious community. It is for this reason that the New Age Movement and the Eastern religions are so appealing to this postmodern generation. These people are seeking to experience the reality of God, through the reflection of the life of His Son and the powerful demonstration of the presence of the Holy Spirit in the community of Christian believers. Ellen White says, "the world will be convinced, not by what the pulpit teaches, but by what the church lives. The minister in the desk announces the theory of the gospel; the practical piety of the church demonstrates its power."[5]

Jewish Hangover

There are very important lessons that we can learn from another people chosen by God to participate in His mission to save the world. When God called Abraham He intended, through him and his descendants (the Jewish nation), to bless the whole world with a fuller knowledge of Himself.[6] However, instead of gratefully and freely sharing the blessing of Jehovah with their surrounding neighbors and the world, they isolated themselves in their walled-off communities and selfishly tried to confine all the benefits of heaven to Israel. Sadly enough, Jewish relations to the rest of the world appear to be very much the same today.

During the ministry of Jesus Christ, the Jews flaunted their "choseness" to all the surrounding nations as a badge of distinction, greatness, and superiority. They based their identity and national status on their historical and biological connection to Abraham. Nothing else really mattered—not the weightier matters of the law (judgment, mercy, and faith[7]), not neighborly relations, not even the Son of God.[8] Being Abraham's seed was the pinnacle of Jewish existence, and the final settlement of every argument with their surrounding neighbors.

Over and over again, Jesus tried to tear down the dividing walls between the Jews and the Gentile world, consistently displaying God's eternal purpose to save all mankind, regardless of color, race, creed, or any other human distinction. This was the case with the woman at Jacob's well (John 4), and the Syrophoenician woman who pleaded with Jesus for the life of her daughter (Mark 7:24-30).[9] Even though Jesus validated the Jewish claim of being Abraham's seed (John 8:37), He also repudiated them for using that claim as a cover for all their evil deeds. He said: "If you were truly Abraham's children, then you would do the works of Abraham—you would follow his example, do as Abraham did. But now [instead] you are wanting and seeking to kill Me, a Man Who has told you the truth which I have heard from God. This is not the way Abraham did" (John 8:39, 40, *The Amplified Bible*). Additionally, John the Baptist reminded the Jews that God was able to raise up seed to Abraham from the lifeless stones under their feet (Luke 3:7-9). Ultimately, the Jews committed their greatest atrocity by rejecting and crucifying the Chosen One of God, upon whom the whole Jewish religious economy rested and to whom all their ceremonies pointed.

Some of us may not readily admit that there are some marked similarities between the Jews and us, but they are there. Just as they were chosen and called of God, so are we. Just as they were blessed of God, so are we. Just as they based their identity on their claim to be Abraham's seed (and they were), so do we on our claim to be the remnant seed of the woman of Revelation 12:17. Just as the Jews took pride in rehearsing their history, so do we in our denominational history.

However, the Jewish appeal to Abraham as the source of their identity appears to be more biological and historical, and less spiritual and relational with regard to the Messiah and the covenant. How do we measure up on this point? Are we espousing our claim to remnancy as a mere historical fact that can be supported by Scripture? Are we flaunting it as a badge of greatness, superiority, and the final settlement of all religious argument with other Protestant denominations and the rest of the world? Mrs. White would remind us that "the badge of Christianity is not an outward sign, not the wearing of a cross or a crown, but it is that which reveals the union of man with God. By the power of His grace manifested in the transformation of character, the world is to be convinced that God has sent His Son as its Redeemer. No other influence that can surround the human soul has such power as the influence of an unselfish life. The strongest argument in favor of the gospel is a loving and lovable Christian."[10]

So what does being the remnant really mean to us, and why do we go out of the way to prove we are who we say we are? Are we reflecting in our lifestyle, behavior, and social relations (or lack thereof) that we are the remnant and that nothing else matters – not the weightier matters of the law (love, justice, compassion, mercy); not neighborliness, not racism or ethnocentrism, not sexual immorality, not worldliness, not partiality or dishonesty? I sometimes wonder what Jesus or John the Baptist might say about our claim to be the remnant people of God today? Perhaps Jesus might say, "If you are the remnant then you will do the works of the remnant and bring forth fruits of righteousness; but why do you still lie, and hate, and discriminate against, and defraud one another? This is not the way the people of the remnant would act." John the Baptist might remind us that God is able to raise up remnant seed to the woman (His Church) from the unconverted world and/or other religious communities.

In other words, remnancy is totally and completely God's call, not ours.[11]

Just as Paul reminded the Jews that they are not all Israel which are of Israel, neither are all children simply because they are the seed of Abraham,[12] we must be reminded that we are not all remnant who are of the remnant, neither are we all true children of God because we are Seventh-day Adventists (seed of the woman of Revelation 12:17). Ellen White says, "if we have the spirit of Christ we shall work as He worked; we shall catch the very ideas of the Man of Nazareth and present them to the people. If, in the place of formal professors and unconverted ministers, we were indeed followers of Christ we would present the truth with such meekness and fervor, and would so exemplify it in our lives, that the world would not be *continually questioning whether we believe what we profess*. The message borne in the love of Christ, with the *worth of souls constantly before us*, would win even from worldlings the decision: *"They are like Jesus"*[13] (italics mine).

I believe that this is what remnancy is all about—reflecting Jesus Christ fully (by proclamation and lifestyle) to the world. It is not about our ability (above other Protestants) to establish historical and biblical data about our origin (important as that is to our existence as a people), but about the living, unqualified and untainted witness that our community of faith has a dynamic, fruitful relationship with Jesus Christ—evidenced in unconditional love, genuine "comm-unity," and selfless service. Like the early church from which we have historically emerged—hence the significance of our claim to remnancy—we ought to be the living reflection of our Founder, Jesus Christ. This reflection must be so clear and so contagious that our present generation, like the people in Antioch, can unequivocally recognize us first as Christians, not just Adventist, Remnant, or any other labeling.

I firmly agree with Ellen White that when we, as a believing community, can personify the spirit and character of Jesus Christ in our daily associations, we can win even from the secular, unchurched world the declaration: "They are like Jesus."[14] [They *must* be the remnant people of God].

Evaluating Motive: Christ and Us

There appears to be a marked difference between the way Christ approached God's mission and the way we approach ours. Christ's mission focus was absolutely clear, and He allowed nothing and no one to detract Him from it. Over and over again, He stated His mission in terms that His hearers could understand: *"For the Son of man is come to seek and to save that which was lost"* (Luke 19:10); *"The Spirit of the Lord is upon me, for he hath anointed me to preach the gospel to the poor; he hath sent me to heal the broken-hearted, to preach deliverance to the captives, and recovering of sight to the blind, to set at liberty them that are bruised, to preach the acceptable year of the Lord"* (Luke 4:18, 19); *"For I came down from heaven, not to do mine own will, but the will of him that sent me"* (John 6:38).

Christ came, not to represent Himself, but His Father in heaven. He did not come to *prove* that He was the promised Messiah (as important as that was). Christ already knew who He was, and never once gave a positive response to any request for Him to prove that fact. Twice in the wilderness of temptation, Satan asked Christ to prove that He was the Son of God,[1] but in either case He repulsed the crafty foe with the unerring *"It is written"* (Matthew 4:4, 7, and 10).

When the Pharisees and Sadducees requested of Christ to show them a sign of His Messiahship and authority,[16] He forthrightly rebuked them and left their presence. Judas hoped to force Christ (through betrayal) to *prove* He was the Kingly Messiah, the hope of all Israel, but was tragically devastated when Christ allowed Himself to be taken captive and led away to unlawful judgment. Then, when Jesus appeared before Herod as the condemned prisoner, Scripture says that Herod was very glad to see Him because he had heard of Jesus' fame and hoped to satisfy his curiosity regarding Him by having Jesus perform a miracle in his presence (Luke 23:8). Scripture confirms that Christ answered Herod not even one word (Luke 23:9). Finally, on the cross, Christ was challenged to *prove* He was the Son of God by saving Himself from its painful, terrible death. However, Christ chose to complete His mission and died as the Lamb of God to take away the sin of the world.

Throughout the Savior's earthly existence Satan dogged His every step with the powerful, overwhelming temptation to *prove* He was the Son of God, but without any success. Ellen White clearly points out, "had Christ complied with the suggestion of the enemy, Satan would still have said, Show me a sign that I may believe you to be the Son of God. *Evidence* would have been worthless to break the power of rebellion in his heart."[17] If Christ did not have a definitive understanding of who He was, and for what purpose He came, who knows whether or not He would have yielded to the powerful temptation to *prove* that He came from God. The fact that Christ had no doubt about who He was released Him from the need to *prove* Himself to anyone. He simply lived out who He was in His daily association with men and women. He did not try to prove He was the promised Messiah; He simply lived out the role of the Messiah (Luke 4:18).

While a discouraged, hopeless prisoner in the dungeon of Herod, John the Baptist sent his disciples to Jesus with the question: "Are you the one, or do we look for another?"[18] This was the same John who, only a short time before, had pointed to Jesus and said: "*Behold the Lamb of God, which taketh away the sin of the world*" (John 1:29). Now tired, lonely, despondent, and desperately afraid, frail humanity reaches out to catch (as it were) the last straw. Jesus was heart-broken at John's inquiry, and longed to comfort His faithful disciple and forerunner, but John, too, must pass the acid test: "Who do you say that I am?" (Mark 8:29 NASB). Christ appeared to pay not regard to question of John's disciples, but continued to minister to the suffering masses that were all around Him. In wonder of His silence at their query, and in awe at the healing grace that emanated from His presence, these questioning disciples were strangely drawn to follow Christ all through the day. At the end of the day, Christ called them to Himself and finally answered their question with the words: *"Go and show John again those things which ye do hear and see"* (Matthew 11:4, 5). Scripture does not record John's response to the testimonies he heard from his disciples, but I would like to believe that John's confidence in Jesus as the promised Messiah was rekindled and that he went to his death as a victor.

However, the very important point that must not be overlooked here is that the *evidence* of Christ's messiahship was not the product of persuasive, intellectual arguments, but the invincible, indisputable power of His consistent godly life, expended in love and service to others. Even when this life ended on the cross, the hardened sinners, who performed the execution, uttered the ultimate truth: *"Truly this was the Son of God"* (Matthew 27:54).

I am sorely afraid that in our mission enterprise we have not completely followed the example of the Master Teacher. Jesus' vision of His mission was very clear. He came to represent the Father and to save the lost. What about our vision of our mission? Christ spent His entire life lifting up God, the Father, portraying His unconditional love and mercy for sinners. On the other hand, we spend more time trying to prove and defend our remnant position than in lifting up Jesus and portraying His love to the world. Our mission must be clear and must be understood by all our people. Far too much of our energy and resources are spent in trying to prove to the world that we are God's remnant, instead of speaking of and portraying the glorious majesty of Jesus Christ as the ONLY SAVIOR OF THE WORLD.

If we cannot convince the world regarding who we are after these many years of presenting biblical and historical data about that identity, then when will we ever succeed in doing so? What is it that the world is still missing? I am of the opinion that the real problem lies not in our inability to adequately prove that we are the remnant, but in our serious lack of spiritual power to live like the remnant people of God. Ellen White is worth being repeated here: "The world will be convinced, not by what the pulpit teaches, but by what the church lives. The minister in the desk announces the theory of the gospel; the practical piety of the church demonstrates its power."[19] This lack of power on our part is mainly due to our intractable focus on ourselves, and the promotion of our denominational ambitions; instead of centering our focus on Christ, who ALONE can reproduce the character of the remnant in us. Ellen White reveals, "had there been more lifting up of Jesus and less extolling the minister, *more praise rendered to the Author of truth and less to its messengers [EVEN THE REMNANT]*, we would occupy a more favorable position before God than we do today"[20] (italics mine).

Missing the Mark

The message to Laodicea[21] (with whom we have traditionally associated ourselves) is a painful reminder of the fact that we are too full of ourselves, with very little room for Christ. The Faithful and True Witness (Jesus Christ) says that we have a gross misconception of ourselves, and of our accomplishments. He comments: *"You say I am rich and have become wealthy, and have need of nothing, and you **do not know** that you are wretched and miserable and poor and blind and **naked**[22]"* (Rev. 3:17 NASB, emphasis mine). Through His straight, pointed testimony, Christ chips away at every ounce of our denominational pride, self-proclaimed glory, and religious elitism, and gives us His uncompromising, unequivocal reality check. He exposes the nerve center of our denominational mind-set and socio-religious culture that tends to place Adventism at the center of the world, and reveals the true nature of our physical and moral worth. In this very uncomfortable scenario, what really matters is not how we see, or what we think about ourselves, but only what Jesus sees and thinks about us. We compare ourselves with other Protestant denominations and think we are the religious elite, but Jesus says we are bankrupt in spite of all our accomplishments. Our bankruptcy lies not in the measure or greatness of our accomplishments, but in the emptiness of our boast. That boast exposes the inherent human weakness characterized by a disposition that constantly seeks for preeminence and the approbation of others. However, as a people, we must tread very softly here, lest we find ourselves under heaven's displeasure of trying to "steal" Christ's thunder (glory). It is dangerously foolish to have the Savior of our souls compete with the savior of our success.[23]

Listening to Wise Counsel

Christ challenges our selfish preoccupations with the call to come back to Him as the ultimate solution to our spiritual dilemma. "Buy of Me," He says (for there is no one else), "gold tried in the fire, that you may become rich" (Revelation 3:18). This gold represents genuine faith in Christ, motivated by love for Christ, and purifies the soul of the believer.[24] It portrays complete reliance on Jesus (not our remnant heritage, our organizational greatness, or our incontrovertible message) as our Surety and our Source of Salvation. It is also characterized by a love that flows out of a genuine connection to Him, embracing all people (regardless of race, ethnicity, lifestyle, religion, etc.), because He is an abiding presence in our midst.

Christ also invites us to replace our earthly rags of self-righteousness and "better-than-thou-ness" with the righteousness that only He can provide. Nothing else will suffice. His righteousness and greatness alone must be manifested in, and be proclaimed by, His people. These are not just external phenomena that can easily be conformed to, under the pressure of a *denominational social culture* (that is, the denominational criteria for being a member in good and regular standing); but these are internal life characteristics reproduced by the very mind and spirit of the living Christ abiding in the soul. This is the legacy of the new covenant—that form of righteousness that springs from the heart. Christ says that if we purchase (without money or price, but through complete surrender) this righteousness from Him, He will not reveal the shame and nakedness of our vain profession that we hold so dear (Revelation 3:18). A revelation of this manner would have such devastating effects upon the fair name we try so desperately to protect that it would produce a terrible shaking of confidence within Adventism. Our self-righteous profession will become so apparent to an on-looking world that it would humble our denominational pride and precipitate a broken, contrite community, who, by experience, knows and embraces Christ as the *only* source and assurance of their righteousness, as the *only* hope and security of their salvation, and as the *only* reason and focus of their boast.

Additionally, Christ wants to clear our spiritual vision by cleansing and changing our hearts (thought processes). Experience has shown that what a person sees does not depend so much on what is in his/her line of vision, but on what he/she has in his/her heart (mind). A person's mind can color any situation. We tend to see people and situations not as they are, but as we are. Therefore Jesus wants to clear our vision by changing our hearts, and this can only happen as we keep our eyes focused on His righteous character and yield our wills to the powerful, converting influence of His Spirit. Christ promises to anoint our eyes with celestial eye salve to counteract our spiritual blindness regarding ourselves, our mission, and the lost world (Revelation 3:18).

This heavenly anointing will give us clear spiritual discernment and vision: (1) *to see* ourselves in the light of the righteous character of Jesus Christ (for without His righteousness we are utterly worthless); (2) *to see* the task of mission as Christ saw it (not to prove our calling to the world, or glorify ourselves, but to glorify Him as we seek to win the lost); and (3) *to see* all men and women as Christ sees them (as people in need of His love and salvation, regardless of their life situation, color, race, ethnicity, or any other human distinction).

Christ Wants In

In His urgent attempt to arrest the attention of His last day people, Christ portrays Himself as standing outside *the door* of a person's soul, knocking and seeking entrance (Revelation 3:20). While this letter to the Laodiceans (Revelation 3:14) addresses the entire church, Christ is seeking for the individual attention of the members who make up the body of believers. In a collective sense, however, Christ is standing outside *the door* of Laodicea (a symbolism of a mental and religious mind-set preoccupied by pride, self-aggrandizement, and earthly kingdom glory) seeking entrance to *the soul* of His church. He wants *IN* on all that goes on in the community of faith. He is not satisfied to be just a figurehead Savior and Lord. He wants to be the ONLY HEAD and controlling influence of the body of believers. He wants the central spot in the heart of His church. Every thought, decision, and action that occur in the body must be controlled by Him, and bring glory ONLY to Him.

While as a community we have not abandoned Christ altogether, we have not made Him the central figure in our life and mission. It is no secret that the glories of our accomplishments as a religious denomination, the pride of our historical heritage, the uniqueness of our doctrinal position, and the overriding desire to prove our remnant legitimacy (which we hope will extend the border of Adventism and swell our numbers) have consumed our attention, our energies, and our resources. Therefore Christ sends us this shocking, wake-up call that soberly reminds us that God's mission is not about us—our remnancy (as important to us as this may be), and our glorious exploits (irrespective of what the numbers may say). Rather, God's mission is ALL about Christ and His power to save (for He alone can justify any sinner), His power to keep (for He alone can sanctify the unrighteous soul of the born-again sinner), and His glory to proclaim (for He ALONE is worthy to be praised). We dare not steal Christ's thunder!

So Christ is knocking. The message to Laodicea does not reveal whether or not *the door* was open for Jesus to gain entrance and access to the heart of His church, but it does portray His willingness to hold sweet communion with those in the body who choose to open the door of their hearts to Him. There is no finality to this message because it is still very much applicable to us today. Christ is still pleading and knocking to gain full access to *the soul* of His church. It is in heeding the counsel of the Faithful and True Witness to return to Jesus as the source our righteousness, our love, our vision, our success, and our boast, that we would be prepared to proclaim with power and persuasion the three angels' messages of Revelation 14:6-12.

These messages were not given in order to validate the identity of the ones who proclaim them. Rather, they were given to in order to extend God's last call of mercy—through the cross—to a soon-to-perish world. The everlasting gospel, which embraces the messages proclaimed by these three angels of Revelation, portrays Jesus' saving work on behalf of sinners. The end product of our proclamation and the Christ-saving work is a people whose life and experience reflect that of their Savior. They are the true patience of the saints, who keep all the commandments of God (not just being obsessed with 4th commandment) and possess the true faith of Jesus.[25] They are God's remnant to the glory and praise of their Redeemer, Jesus Christ.

I am afraid that in our evangelism we often hasten to the end of these beautiful messages (Revelation 14:12) in order to drive home the point that the Seventh-day Adventist Church fits the bill as God's remnant people, and just as often, fail to show how Jesus is saving His people through these messages. As a matter of fact, in our presentation of these messages we tend to focus more on judgment (often condemnation over acquittal), the sins of Babylon, the Beast and his mark, than on the love of Jesus and His way of salvation in this judgment hour. Thus, what should have been portrayed as good news (the everlasting gospel), often comes across to the hearers as bad news.

We need to be constantly reminded that the grand central theme of these messages is Christ Our Righteousness and not who is the remnant. In this regard, Ellen White said: "The end is near! We have not a moment to lose! Light is to shine forth from God's people in clear, distinct rays, bringing *Jesus before the churches and before the world.* . . . If through the grace of Christ His people will become new bottles, He will fill them with the new wine. God will give *additional light, and old truths will be recovered, and replaced in the framework of truth*; and wherever the laborers go, they will triumph. As Christ's ambassadors, they are to search the Scriptures, to seek for the truths that have been hidden beneath the rubbish of error. And every ray of light received is to be communicated to others. ***One interest will prevail, one subject will swallow up every other, Christ our righteousness.*** . . . 'I am the Lord which exercise lovingkindness, judgment, and righteousness in the earth: for in these things I delight, saith the Lord.' This is what needs to be brought into . . . all our churches. God wants every soul to turn to the first love. He wants all to have the gold of faith and love, so that they can draw from the treasure to impart to others who need it"[26] (emphasis mine).

The glory of humanity, even the glory of Adventism must be buried in the dust, so that the eternal, effulgent glory of the Son of righteousness may draw ALL men (Christians and non-Christians, church and unchurched, religious and secular, saint and sinner) to the Savior. The praise and glory of Christ alone must form not only the source of our motivation, but also the center and glory of our boast.

Re-Thinking Our Mission Methods

The message to Laodicea represents a clarion call for us, God's remnant community, to re-think our calling and our mission. If we truly believe that God has called us to be His last-day people, with a special message for this end time, then let us accept and embrace that fact and move on to what God has called us to be and to do. Like Jesus, the Messiah, let us not be sidetracked by futile cerebral engagements, trying to prove what we already know, and what the carnal world may never fully understand; and let us be committed to proving who Jesus is by living like the remnant people of God. "By *this* all men *will* know that you are My disciples, if you have love for one another" (John 13:35, NASB italics mine).

In His prayer for His disciples and for us, Jesus uttered these profound words: "Neither for these alone do I pray–it is not for their sake only that I make this request–but also for all those who will ever come to believe in Me through their word and teaching; So that they all may be one [just] as You, Father, are in Me and I in You, that they also may be one in Us, so *that the world may believe and be convinced that You have sent Me*" (John 17:20, 21, *The Amplified Bible*, italics mine).

As we re-think our approach to mission, we must be open to the Person of the Holy Spirit, who is earnestly waiting to do new and exciting things among and through us. Paramount among these is the clear revelation of our utter unworthiness to participate in God's mission apart from the righteous character of His Son; our total inadequacy to fulfill God's mission without the power of Christ through His Spirit; and our desperate need to earnestly humble our hearts and minds to the Lordship of Jesus Christ. Mission must begin with Christ, be sustained by Christ, and must end in Christ. In order for us to pursue God's mission in God's way, there must be a willingness on our part to (1) embrace the mind of Christ, (2) live the life of Christ, (3) daily submit to the Spirit of Christ, and (4) incorporate the methods of Christ in our mission practice.

Embracing the Mind of Christ

This is first and foremost, because as a man thinks in his heart, so is he (Proverbs 23:7). We are admonished by the apostle Paul: "*Let this mind be in us which also was in Christ Jesus*" (Philippians 2:5 italics mine). How desperately we need the mind of Christ to replace our mind-set that continually gets in the way of God's mission. When the mind of Christ possesses us, we will begin to think about God's mission the way Christ did; we will begin to see and love people the way Christ did; and we will not be so reticent in mingling with and serving them the way Christ did. Christ in us, the hope of glory, will motivate and constrain us to bring hope and salvation to a dying world.

Christ's Reputation and Ours

In speaking about the mind of Christ, Paul says that He made Himself of no reputation in order to save mankind. His mission and passion were to seek and to save the lost. He sought them wherever they were, whoever they were, and however they were, until they were found – and He saved them. Nothing was more important to Christ than this central task. He allowed nothing and no one to get in the way of His mission of seeking and saving sinners. No! Not His reputation (for He gave up equality with God and the adoration of angels that praised Him, to be numbered with transgressors who rejected, despised, and crucified Him); not the glories of heaven (for He left those glories to walk in the valley of the shadow of death); not his Kingly robe and star-studded crown (for He gave those up for borrowed clothes and a crown of thorns); not even His own life (for He accepted the death which was ours so that we could receive the life which is His[27]). Christ paid no attention to those who attacked His reputation because of His commitment to save sinners (See Luke 5:30-32; 15). He, Who is equal with God, did not make that equality (that is, His Reputation) something to be grasped after or to be protected; but made Himself of no reputation (by becoming a man), stepping out of His comfort zone, into our conflict zone, in order to bring us into His saving zone.

It is very disconcerting when we, as followers of Jesus, allow our "reputation" (individually and collectively) to get in the way of God's mission to save sinners. There are many among us who would rather not see or have in our fellowship certain sinners (especially those whose lifestyle, race, color, ethnicity and gender are different from theirs), for fear of having our comfort zone disturbed, or our reputation marred. Moreover, some professed Christian communities would rather leave secular, unchurched people to die in their sins than to adjust their way of doing church in order to reach them.

One of Christianity's greatest undoings is its un-Christlike attitude towards people whose lifestyle runs against social norms of everyday society. Homosexuals and lesbians, drug-dealers and drug-users, pimps and prostitutes, child molesters and pornographers, rapists and robbers (to name a few) are often treated as though they are sold to Satan and are outside the pales of God's grace or plan of salvation. Yet Scripture portrays Christ as being the Friend and Savior of publicans and sinners.[28] As a matter of fact, Jesus once told the self-righteous Scribes and Pharisees that prostitutes and publicans[29] would enter the kingdom before them (See Matthew 21:31). I can only wonder what Jesus would say about the pharisaism of modern Christianity.

The Scribes and Pharisees projected a reputation that they did not really possess. They appeared righteous in their dress and their deportment, but their speech and actions betrayed the true nature of their character. Jesus said of them, *"For you are like whitewashed tombs which on the outside appear beautiful, but inside they are full of dead men's bones and all uncleanness. Even so you too outwardly appear righteous to men, but inwardly you are full of hypocrisy and lawlessness"* (Matthew 23:27, 28, NASB).

In post-modern Christendom, many believers have taken the stance to orient their lives around protecting their reputation at the eternal expense of the lost. While preservation of character is a good and healthy spiritual practice, when that preservation inhibits us from interacting with lost men and women for the kingdom of God, then that character preservation becomes self-serving and spiritually defective. Jesus said: "He who lives to save his life [*and I dare say reputation*] shall lose it, and whosoever shall lose his life [*and reputation*] for My sake and the gospel shall save it" (Mark 8:35, italics mine).

There are times when erring, but REPENTANT, children of God are cut off from the fellowship of believers in order to protect the "reputation" and "fair name" of the church. While it is necessary for the church to be uncompromising in dealing with sin, it must also be compassionate and just in dealing with REPENTANT sinners in the mind and spirit of Christ. The tendency in many Christian communities is to focus more on the sin committed and its possible repercussions on the image and reputation of the church, than on the attitude (even if it is broken and contrite) and needs of the erring one. However, Jesus our example, Who had all the IMAGE and REPUTATION to protect (for He alone is holy and righteous), never disassociated Himself from erring sinners in order to preserve His "fair name." He, Whose name is the FAIREST OF TEN THOUSAND, never withdrew from broken sinners seeking Him. Rather, He said: "All that the Father giveth me shall come to me, and *him that cometh to me I shall in NO WISE cast out*" (John 6:37, italics mine). I interpret NO WISE to mean without any qualification or supposition. Any sinner (regardless of the deed) that comes to Jesus WILL receive His pardon and acceptance. Can the true followers of Christ do any less?

The scribes and Pharisees constantly accused Jesus for being in the company and fellowship of sinners. We must be put in remembrance that it was His "fair name"—JESUS (which actually means Savior of sinners - Mathew 1:23) that gave Him the reputation that "this man welcomes sinners and eats with them" (Luke 15:2). How many of our congregations would really like to have a reputation like that? There are many Christians who go around flashing their WWJD (What Would Jesus Do) badges of Christianity, but who recoil from working, or refuse to work, with Jesus in befriending and loving sinners for the kingdom of God.

Bill Hull reminds us, "Jesus ministered with both feet in the [*real*] world. He launched out into his world without being overly concerned about getting soiled. We, too, need to be willing to risk criticism from others in order to reach those in need. Such a commitment usually involves social interaction with those who practice different ethics. But as followers of the One who did not compromise, we are called to reach out to the people who are in need, breaking down the barriers by spending time with them. This may entail going out to dinner with non-Christian neighbors rather than heading off to the Sunday school class party. People who are more concerned with their religious reputation than with the welfare of others will not understand, for they have chosen sacrifice over mercy. If this perspective sounds radical, that's because it is! The reason it is radical rather than typical is that, in evangelism, the Church has often followed more in the steps of the Pharisees than in the steps of Jesus"[30] (italics mine).

    Jesus Christ was very clear when He said, "except our *righteousness* exceeds the *righteousness* of the Scribes and the Pharisees we shall in *NO WISE* enter into the kingdom of heaven. (Matthew 5:20, emphasis mine). Jesus' "NO WISE" qualification appears here again, but this time it is an expression of His unqualified rejection. What a contrast to the open acceptance Christ gives to the unpretentious, broken sinner who comes to Him for forgiveness and cleansing! The "righteousness" of the Scribes and Pharisees was only an external "righteousness" that craved the recognition and approval of men; one that made the possessor feel that he/she was better than other sinners (See Luke 18:9-14); one that was void of compassion for sinners, and sought to protect itself by either isolation from, or rejection of, sinners. It was this same form of "righteousness" that eventually put to death the RIGHTEOUS SON OF GOD. What a paradox! What strange things this form of "righteousness" will do, even in the name of God!

What type of righteousness do we display when we have to deal with lost sinners on the outside and fallen sinners on the inside of the community of faith? Is it the true righteousness of Christ or the "righteousness" of the Scribes and Pharisees? It seems rather ironic that we (forgiven sinners), who are without any reputation (except that which we have on account of Jesus ALONE), try to protect what we do not really possess, when it has to do with our fallen brothers and sisters in the faith, or reaching out to "certain" sinners. We seem sorely afraid of spiritual contamination by association (if such a thing really exists), and worry that forgiveness and acceptance will lead to spiritual anarchy. To the contrary, forgiveness and acceptance give the repentant sinner hope and a reason to change. Romans 2:4 says that it is through God's goodness (for example, His forgiveness and acceptance) that sinners are motivated to repentance—that is, exercise godly sorrow for and a turning away from sin. As we participate in the carrying forth of God's mission, it is our duty and spiritual calling to mirror the attitude of Christ to all types of sinners and trust in His name and His power to save and keep them.

Living the Life of Christ

It is by embracing and incorporating Christ's life that we are able to rightly reflect His image and message to the world. Philip Samaan suggests that "in our fervor to do the works of Christ we must, first of all, focus on Christ, and make sure that we have His spirit in all that we do in his service. We need to closely follow His way to true spirituality and allow such an experience to transform everything for Him. After all, we must possess what we profess and perform. Our duty to Christ must ever be linked to our devotion to Christ."[31]

The paradigm shift in our mission practice must incorporate moving from the preoccupation with the skills and abilities of our organization and individuals who manage it, to a focus on the beauty, holiness, and attractiveness of the character of Christ. By beholding we become changed into His likeness for His glory. Ellen White says, "Christ is sitting for His portrait in every disciple. Every one God has predestinated to be 'conformed to the image of his Son' (Romans 8:29). In every one Christ's longsuffering love, His holiness, meekness, mercy, and truth are to be manifested to the world."[32]

Wayne McDill reminds us, "we do not become effective at influencing men for Christ by concentrating on ourselves and our growing skills. Our effectiveness will never depend on that. The key will always be our immediate, personal relationship with our Lord as we follow him."[33] "When the disciples came forth from the Savior's training, they were no longer ignorant and uneducated. They had become like Him in mind and character, and men took knowledge of them that they had been with Jesus."[34] It is the power of this manifestation of Christ's life in us, born out of daily communion with Him, that makes us effective witnesses and fruit-bearing disciples. Ellen White points out, "when the love of Christ is enshrined in the heart, like sweet fragrance it cannot be hidden. Its holy influence will be felt by all with whom we come in contact."[35] This is our most urgent need, the manifestation of which would give potency to our verbal witness for Christ in these last days.

Ellen White was very careful in pointing out that "nothing is more needed in our work than the practical results of communion with God . . . His peace in the heart will shine forth in the countenance. It will give to the voice a persuasive power. Communion with God will ennoble the character and the life. Men will take knowledge of us, as of the first disciples, that we have been with Jesus. This will impart to the worker a power that nothing else can give. Of this power he must not allow himself to be deprived."[36]

Submitting to the Spirit of Christ

Mission evangelism (personal or public) is a spiritual activity, and trying to conduct it without the Person and power of the Holy Spirit is like trying to generate light from incandescent lamps without electricity. The ministry of Christ was anointed by the presence and power of the Holy Spirit (Luke 4:18, 19). Moreover, Christ emphasized the intimate relationship between receiving the Holy Spirit and witnessing, when He commissioned His disciples to wait in Jerusalem for the promised blessing (Acts 1:8). It seems rather incongruous and somewhat disturbing that as a post-Pentecost denomination, we speak so little about the presence, authority, and ministry of the Holy Spirit within the body of Christ. This third Person of the Godhead has not received the level of recognition and prominence that He deserves in our community of faith. How can we ever hope to experience the latter rain when we hardly ever speak of, or commune with, the Divine Comforter?

In prior years we were used to having *one-week* of Holy Spirit emphasis throughout the world of Adventism. Imagine living in the dispensation of the Holy Ghost and devoting only one week out of an entire year to talk about, and create a living consciousness of Him. Now the *one-week* Holy Spirit emphasis has altogether disappeared from our yearly calendars, and what do we have left? Nothing! Ellen White asks: "Since this is the means by which we are to receive power, why do we not hunger and thirst for the gift of the Spirit? Why do we not talk of it, pray for it, and preach concerning it?"[37]

This was not the way of the early church after Pentecost. The Book of Acts postures the Holy Spirit as a living and active Presence in the community of believers. In my view, this Book is more about the Acts of the Holy Spirit than is it about the Acts of the Apostles. The Holy Spirit was everywhere, and was recognized, respected, and related to throughout the believing community.[38] Of course some may be tempted to say: "Well, the Holy Spirit was an active, living Presence in the early church simply because it was the time of His inaugural entrance into the world, but it is not so now." I believe that the mighty demonstrations of the Holy Spirit among the people of God were not simply a signal to the world and believers that He was (and is) here. These supernatural manifestations were also undeniable signs of what could happen when the believing community recognizes the Holy Comforter for Who He is, and is open and prepared to receive Him as the ONLY reality and guarantee of Jesus, the risen One.

I am convinced that the upper room experience of the early disciples, which drew the mighty presence of the Holy Spirit, was also diffused into the believing community and generated the same response from the Divine Comforter. Scripture says, "And all they that believed were together, and had all things in common; they would sell their possessions and goods, and distributed the proceeds to all, as any had need. Day by day, as they spent much time together in the temple, they broke bread at home and ate their food with glad and generous hearts, praising God and having the goodwill of all the people. And day by day the Lord added to their number those who were being saved" (Acts 2:44-47, NRSV). As the remnant of that early Pentecostal Church, God's last day people must be possessors of that same spiritual, communal, kingdom-shaking heritage. Our confession must move beyond the formal, intellectual and theological to the organic, ontological and experiential, bringing the reality and the power of the living Christ to a hungry, hurting world.

I firmly agree with Mrs. White that "when *we* bring our hearts into unity with Christ, and our lives into harmony with His work, the Spirit that fell on the disciples on the day of Pentecost will fall on us"[39] (italics mine). But Satan has gained some advantage on us with regard to the Divine Gift of the Holy Spirit. While evangelistic programs exist in abundance across the landscape of Adventism, the accompanying converting, miracle-working and fruit-bearing power of the Holy Spirit is not readily seen.

Many times we discredit what the Spirit may actually be doing in other religious communities, as though His super-natural activity is limited to the borders of Adventism. Yet, God is no respecter of persons or denominations. The measure of His gifts flows in proportion to our willingness and capacity to receive. I am of the opinion that we shy away from talking too much about Jesus and the Holy Ghost (if there could ever be too much of either) simply because other Protestant denominations place a lot of emphasis on them. On one occasion, I engaged one of our pastors about making Jesus Christ more central in his preaching and evangelism, and he was very forthcoming in telling me that he did not want to sound like one of "those" Sunday preachers, talking only Jesus, but saying nothing.

While I was a student at the seminary, I was taking

a class on the gospel of John. One day I asked my professor the following questions: "If we believe that we are living in the dispensation of the Holy Spirit, and that He brings the reality and all blessings of Christ to us, why is it that we do not talk to, and about, Him much more than we do? Why is it that we still pray and ask Jesus to send His Holy Spirit and He is already here waiting for us to approach Him? Why is there only passing reference to Him in all our prayers, our preaching and our teaching?" I was made to understand that we have no real need to approach the Holy Spirit in prayer, and that any time people begin to become obsessed about the Holy Spirit, it is because they have some sort of moral problem. Needless to say, I was truly disappointed by the reply and never made mention of the subject again in that class.

In our attempt to preserve "our identity," and to disassociate ourselves from other Protestants and their views on these subjects (Jesus, the Holy Spirit, miracles of healing), we have de-emphasized them, or shied away from them altogether. Thus, we "throw away the baby with the bath water," and truncate the channels of blessings urgently needed by the believing community. Ellen White says, "if the fulfillment of the promise is not seen as it might be, it is because the promise is not *appreciated* as it should be. . . It is not because of any restriction on the part of God that the riches of His grace do not flow earthward to men"[40] (italics mine). I honestly believe that we need to adjust our attitude and relation to the Divine Comforter so that we can reap the full benefits of His presence in our lives and our mission enterprises.

Instead of reacting to what other religious communities are or are not doing, in order to appear different, we need to be foremost in presenting the truth about the Third Person of the Godhead. The Holy Spirit must be kept as a constant living reality before our people. We desperately need more of Him and not less. We are reminded, "there is no limit to the usefulness of one, who putting self aside makes room for the working of the Holy Spirit upon his heart, and lives a life wholly consecrated to God."[41] Moreover, "the Spirit awaits our demand and reception."[42] I agree with Fish and Conant that "it is not programs we lack; it is power! . . . It is not the imperative of an external command that sends us after the lost; it is the impulse of an indwelling Presence. . . . Behind all successful work for the lost is an inward spiritual impulse; and behind the impulse is the Holy Spirit who reproduces Christ in us."[43]

The time has come for us to take our eyes off what others are (or are not) doing, lift our vision heavenward, and wholeheartedly embrace the Person and Presence of the Holy Spirit. He is our only hope to reproduce the character of Christ in us, and through us, bring the grand climax to the mission of God in the world. We must prayerfully and boldly embrace the spirit of the early church, whose remnant we are! We must follow them in proclamation and in power!

Following the Methods of Christ

Finally, if we are to succeed in fulfilling God's mission, we must have an unswerving commitment to incorporating Christ's methods in personal and public evangelism. Ellen White reminds us, "Christ's method alone will give true success in reaching the people. The Savior mingled with men as one who desired their good. He showed His sympathy for them, ministered to their needs, and won their confidence. Then He bade them, 'Follow Me.'"[44] Building on this invaluable concept, Philip Samaan[45] has done excellent work in extracting five basic principles that encapsulate Christ's way of reaching people for the kingdom of God. I will not attempt to go indepth with these principles here (Saaman has already done so in his book); instead, I will focus our attention on the powerful, logical sequence of Jesus' approach, as follows:

Firstly, Christ *mingled* with people, showing a genuine interest in their well-being. The purpose of His mingling was twofold – (1) to show complete identification with people in their life's situations, and (2) to give them a close up view of God. Samaan says (and I agree), "Christ reached out to people for their own sake—simply because they were who they were, and because people were His first priority."[46] He sought access to their hearts in "a way that made them feel the completeness of His identification with their interests and happiness."[47] The bottom line of this first principle is that if we do not intentionally mingle with people, we cannot influence them for the kingdom of God. Salt that remains in the saltshaker is utterly worthless.

Secondly, Christ *sympathized* with people. He *took the time to listen* to their concerns, *to enter into* their feelings, *to weep* with those who wept, and *to rejoice* with those rejoiced.[48] Paul said that "we do not have a high-priest who is unable to sympathize with our weaknesses, but we have one who in every respect has been tested as we are, yet without sin" (Hebrews 4:15 NRSV). As Christ's followers, our hearts must resonate with His in the same caring, compassionate concern for the fallen, downtrodden, estranged and hurting victims of modern society. People must sense that we are genuinely concerned about them and their private pains and mental strains. McDill believes that "the unbeliever will be much more receptive to the idea that God really cares when he has a Christian friend who has demonstrated that godly care."[49]

Thirdly, Christ took time to *minister* to peoples' needs. Because the Savior understood human nature so well, and took the time to *mingle* with them and *listen* to their concerns, He was able to deliver satisfaction and, ultimately, salvation to them. I am fully aware that this postmodern generation may be preoccupied with needs that are altogether selfish and carnal, without any reference to God. However, *we may never be able to touch people in the area of their deepest need without first touching them where they think they are hurting.*[50]

Fourthly, Christ *won the confidence* of the people He

mingled with, *sympathized* with, and *ministered* to. It is no surprise, therefore, why people were drawn to Him. They never met anyone who cared for them the way Jesus did. When we demonstrate the same level of care and concern in our daily interactions with people (those who are like us, and those unlike us), they will be drawn to us, for we too will have *earned* their confidence. These people will no longer be strangers, but friends.

Lastly, Christ *invited* His friends *to follow* Him. This was not an invitation to wander around Palestine with Him. It was an unmistakable call to discipleship—a challenge to be like Him Who called them, and a commission to go and make disciples of others. As disciples of Jesus Christ, we dare not stop short of building friendships and winning the confidence of people. We are under obligation as ambassadors of heaven to help reconcile these people to God. As reconcilers, we must invite our friends to follow us in the ministry of reconciliation.

Herein lies our strategy for evangelistic success. Jesus was a crowd puller because He was a genuine people lover. Wherever He went, people were drawn to Him. If we follow His example of *mingling, sympathizing,* and *ministering* to people, we will *earn their confidence* and open the door for them to accept our *invitation to follow* us in the service of the King of kings. We must alter our practice of engaging people as STRANGERS with our tracts, surveys, and evangelist paraphernalia when we are planning a campaign. These traditional approaches cost a lot of money, time, and energy, with less than commensurate levels of response from our own people and also from the intended target audiences. If we encourage the body of believers to follow Christ's method of *mingling, sympathizing, ministering to*, and *earning the confidence* of friends and strangers where they live, and work, and play, we will see far more people flowing to our evangelistic meetings and through our church doors. Indeed, Christ's method alone will give true success in reaching people for the kingdom of God.[51]

Notes

1. Bert B. Beach is Director for Inter-Church Relations at the General Conference of Seventh-day Adventists, Silver Spring, MD. This quote was taken from his article "Adventism and Secularization," *Ministry* (April 1996): 22-25.
2. See John 12:32
3. White, *Testimonies to The Church* 5:158.
4. George Knight, Seminary Professor at Andrews University, made this statement in his presentation, "If I Were The Devil," on July 2nd, at the Adventist World Session 2000, in Toronto Canada.
5. White, *Testimonies for the Church* 7:16
6. See Genesis 12:1-4; Galatians 3:6-9.
7. Matthew 23:23.
8. Read John 8:31-59.
9. For more on these examples see chapter 4.
10. Ellen White, *Counsels On Sabbath School Work* (Washington, D.C.: Review and Herald Publishing Association, 1938), 100.
11. See Jon Dybdahl's "It's God's Call," *The Adventist Review* (May 9, 1996):12-14.
12. Romans 9:6-8.
13. White, *Testimonies to The Church* 5:159-60.
14. Ibid.
15. Read Matthew 4:1-7 for a full account of this life and death encounter.
16. See Matthew 12:38-45; Mark 8:11-13.

17. White, *Desire of Ages*, 119.
18. Read the entire account in Matthew 11:2-19
19. White, *Testimonies to The Chruch* 7:16.
20. White, *Testimonies to The Church* 5:159.
21. Read Revelation 3:14-22. *Laodicea* means "a people adjudged" or judgment bound people. We believe that God raised up the Seventh-day Adventist Church to announce the judgment hour message of Rev. 14: 6, 7, to prepare a people for judgement and the second coming of Jesus Christ.
22. Gk. *Gumnos* is translated here as naked of spiritual clothing.
23. Philip G. Samaan, *Christ's Way to Spiritual Growth* (Hagerstown, MD: Review and Herald Publishing Association, 1995), 34.
24. Ellen White, *Christ Object Lessons* (Washington, D.C.: Review and Herald Publishing Association, 1941), 158.
25. Revelation 14:12.
26. Ellen White, *Sons and Daughters of God* (Washington, DC: Review and Herald Publishing Association, 1955), 259.
27. White, *Desire of Ages*, 25.
28. See Matt. 11:19 where Jesus defends rejected sinners. See also John 8:1-11 for the account of the adulterous woman. Also Luke 23:39-43. Here Jesus postponed dying in order to save a dying thief.
29. Publicans were Jewish tax-collectors who were despised and hated by their countrymen because they collected and exacted taxes from their people for the loathed Roman government. Tax collectors were noted for imposing more taxes than were required so that they might more quickly enrich themselves. *Publicans were regarded as traitors, and apostates, defiled by their frequent contacts with pagans, and willing tools of the oppressor. Hence, they were classed with sinners, harlots, and pagans* (Matt 9:11; 21:31; Mark 2:16; Luke 5:27-30; Luke 18:11). [italics mine] See J. D. Douglas and Merrill C. Tenney, eds., *The New International Dictionary of The Bible* (Grand Rapids: Zondervan Publishing House, 1987), 726.
30. Bill Hull, *Jesus Christ Disciple Maker*, (Grand Rapids: Fleming H. Revell, 1994), 111-112.
31. Philip Samaan, *Christ's Way to Spiritual Growth*, 15.
32. White, *Desire of Ages*, 827.
33. Wayne McDill, *Making Friends for Christ* (Nashville: Broadman Press, 1979), 108.
34. White, *Desire of Ages*, 250.
35. Ellen White, *Steps to Christ* (Washington, DC: Review and Herald Publishing Association, 1908), 77.
36. Ellen White, *The Ministry of Healing* (Mountain View, CA: Pacific

Press Publishing Association, 1942), 512.
37. Ellen White, *Acts of The Apostles* (Boise, ID: Pacific Press Publishing Association, 1911), 50.
38. See Acts 2; 4:31-35; 5:1-16; 6:1-7; 13:1-4.
39. White, *Testimonies to The Church* 8:246.
40. Ellen White, *Christian Service* (Hagerstown, MD: Review and Herald Publishing Association, 1947), 252
41. Ibid, 254.
42. Ibid, 252.
43. Roy J. Fish and J. E. Conant, *Every-Member Evangelism for Today* (New York: Harper and Row, 1976), 74-75.
44. White, *The Ministry of Healing*, 143.
45. See his books *Christ's Way of Reaching People* and *Christ's Way of Making Disciples* (Hagerstown, MD: Review and Heralds Publishing Association, 1999) for a very comprehensive treatment of this subject.
46. Ibid, 45
47. White, *Gospel Workers*, 45.
48. White, *Ministry of Healing*, 157.
49. McDill, 65.
50. James A. Ponder, ed. (Nashville: Broadman Press, 1974), 79, 80.
51. White, *The Ministry of Healing*, 143.

Conclusion

*I*n this volume I have taken a very candid look at some of the challenges that confront my church as it engages in God's mission in this post-modern, secular age. What I have presented is not intended to be the final prescription for these challenges, but an alternative point of reference from which we can conduct and sustain our mission enterprise. It is my hope that the information provided in this book will be used to stimulate further thought and creative investigation into a multiplicity of ways to carry out God's mission. I believe that it is in the context of such an enterprising environment that new steps will be taken and new strategies will be implemented to ensure that every nation, kindred, tongue, and people have the opportunity to hear a very clear presentation of the everlasting gospel.

Our claim to "remnancy" poses a major challenge to the mission of the church around the world, especially in an age of growing secularism and post-modernism, where relativism with regard to truth and orthodoxy is fast becoming the norm. However, the church's future mission enterprise must consider the needs of the secular, the unsaved and the unchurched, as well as God's children in "Babylon", such consideration necessitating some adjustment in our thinking and attitude towards these people groups.

There is also room for some measure of openness and dialogue between our ministers and those of other denominations, to reduce heretofore adversarial relationships among the clergy and people. This can create a climate in which information and strategies can be shared on how to approach and win the unchurched and people of non-Christian religions for the kingdom of God. This is not a call for doctrinal compromise or a tainting of the Adventist "image", but there is much that we can learn from the success ventures of other Christian churches. It would be very naive or, more accurately, arrogant to think that God has blessed only the Seventh-day Adventist Church with all there is to know about the *Missio Dei*.

Despite the many challenges facing the church in this present secular age, it dare not relinquish its task to offer hope and salvation to a perishing world. Although modern society does not look to the church as a relevant source of authority today, its voice must be clearly heard above the din and cacophonous distractions of relativism, narcissism, secularism, and whatever else is attempting to shape the thoughts and lives of lost men and women. Since as a community of faith we have a divine mandate to fish for lost people in this corrupt and confused age, we must be in earnest to develop creative ways of engaging them with the good news of the gospel of salvation. I find the following statements by Ellen White very compelling in relating to this important point. She said, "in the cities of today where there is so much to attract and please, the people can be interested by no ordinary efforts. Ministers of God's appointment will find it necessary to put forth extraordinary efforts in order to arrest the attention of the multitudes . . . They must make

CONCLUSION

use of ***every means that can possibly be devised*** for causing the truth to stand out clearly and distinctly."[1] "Let every worker in the Master's vineyard study, plan, devise methods, to reach the people ***where they are.*** We must do something ***out of the common course of things. We must arrest the attention.*** We must be deadly in earnest. We are on the very verge of times of trouble and perplexities that are scarcely dreamed of"[2] (emphasis mine).

When I first read these statements, a number of questions raced through my mind. Are we contented with our present efforts? Are our present methods really arresting the attention of this secular generation? Are we really connecting with our present society? Is this precious message really getting through to the people who need it most—that is, secular, unchurched, unsaved, and non-Christian people? How willing are we, or how far are we willing to go, to put forth the extraordinary efforts that Ellen White says are needed to arrest the attention of the madding multitudes? Are we really willing to use every means that can possibly be devised for causing the truth to stand out clearly and distinctly?

I agree with the servant of God that we live in extraordinary times, and we must be in earnest, and not afraid, to attempt approaches out of the common course of things in order to arrest the attention of lost humanity with the saving gospel of Jesus Christ. Mrs. White further stated, "new methods and new plans will spring from new circumstances. New thoughts will come with new workers who give themselves to the work . . . They will receive plans devised by the Lord Himself."[3]

I believe that now is the time for these new and possibly radical methods to be incorporated into the mainstream mission offensive of our community of faith. The Holy Spirit is eagerly waiting to do a new thing among us, to generate new ways of thinking and acting in our people, to drive us to boldly go where we have not gone before and carry the blood-stained flag of deliverance and salvation to the glory and praise of our soon-coming King. These very critical and decisive moments of earth's history must not be a time for business as usual for the people of God. We must be certain that we do not consume our time or focus our vital resources and energies on in-house issues or the lubrication and maintenance of organizational infrastructure.

Moreover, we must not allow our past accomplishments, present successes, or our perception of our denominational greatness to become stumbling stones in the path of, and distractions from, God's mission and our sacred responsibility to a perishing world. Like the children of Issachar (1Chronicles 12:32), we must understand our times and seek to do what these perilous times demand. Now is not a time to limit ourselves by only the tried and tested methods of yesteryear, while multitudes are rushing headlong into Christless graves. We must release the full potential of the entire body of Christ, to break forth on all fronts—out of the box of traditionalism, as is necessary—and engage the real world for Jesus Christ and the kingdom of God.

CONCLUSION

In a press release immediately following his confirmation as President of the World Church of Seventh-day Adventists, Jan Paulsen said, "the church's focus for the next five years should be directed by mission, not issues."[4] This, I hope, will give mission its rightful place in the life and function of the corporate body of Adventism. It is also my hope that, as we re-think and do God's mission, we will allow the mission, and that alone, to be the paramount factor in addressing the critical issues of organizational structure, mission personnel, mission process and practices, and the criteria for mission evaluation. The best medicine for the existing ills in our community of faith, right now, is not the multiplicity of self-serving programs, but the total commitment and engagement of the whole body of Christ in God's mission to seek and save the lost.

It is time for us to turn our vision and energies upward and outward: upward, so that we can focus our attention on Christ, our Master, Commissioner and Example, and be consumed by His passion for lost humanity; and outward, so that like Christ, we could fulfill God's purpose of reaching the lost with good news of His redemptive plan of reproducing the life of Jesus within everyone who believe the gospel.

Above all, may we never forget that this mission of saving lost people is not ours but God's, and His alone. Nowhere is this more clearly seen than in Christ's parable about the laborers hired to work in their master's vineyard (See Matthew 20:1-16). The punch-line of this picture lesson is the owner's cogent response to the ungrateful indignation of the early hirelings. Unmistakably, it is not the fact that salvation is the free, impartial gift of God to all who would receive it, but the fact that this gift belongs to God, who alone possesses the right to dispense it not only howsoever He wills, but also upon whomsoever it pleases Him to bless. Listen to the owner: "Is it not lawful for me to do what I wish with *what is mine*? Or is your eye envious because I am generous?" (Matthew 20:15, italics mine). God reserves His right as owner over His mission to save the lost.

It is so very easy for us (hirelings) to relate to lost people as though we are the arbiters of their salvation, and if they do not do what we say they cannot enter here nor there. Much too often, the man-made barriers of denominationalism, provincialism, "status quoism", cliquishness, racial and religious intolerance and bigotry subtly weave their way into our mission principles and practices, blocking or diverting the magnanimous flow of God's grace to lost humanity. Through this parable, Christ reminds us that we are all laborers, and not owners, in the Master's vineyard, and as such, we do not have any monopoly whatsoever over the free gift of God to all kinds of sinners.

Mission, therefore, is about what God is doing in the world through myriads of agencies (inside and outside of Adventism) to save His lost children and to vindicate his righteous character before the on-looking universe. It is not about us, our accomplishments, our greatness, and our self-congratulation. God's mission is much more than Adventism, and beckons our "sub-mission" to His overall

CONCLUSION

purpose for lost humanity.

At the center of God's action is the slain Lamb of God (not the remnant), by Whose blood the whole human race is redeemed, and to Whom all the glory belongs. Jesus Christ, the world's Redeemer must be the dominant, dynamic center of our mission philosophy and practice, and as we make it our priority to lift Him up in word and life, He will draw *all* mankind to Himself. For God has "highly exalted Him, and bestowed on Him *the name* which is above every name, that at *the name* of JESUS *every knee should bow*, of those who are in heaven, and on earth, and under the earth, and that *every tongue should confess* that Jesus Christ is LORD, to the glory of God the Father" (Philippians 2:9-11 NASB, emphasis mine). It is of absolutely no consequence whether the knee or the tongue belongs to a Buddhist or a Hindu, a Jew or a Muslim, an agnostic or an infidel, a secular critic or an unchurched person. The mighty, powerful name of JESUS, in synergy with the convicting, converting, creative influence of the Holy Spirit, will bend every inflexible, rebellious knee, and will loose every confused, corrupt tongue, in worship to and praise of the exalted Son of God. Ours is the responsibility to cooperate with God and with heavenly angels in exalting the name of JESUS higher and still higher.

Then, when God's mission in heaven and earth is finally accomplished, one theme will swallow up all others: "Worthy is the Lamb that was slain" (Revelation 5:12). There would be absolutely no room for human acclamations,

boasting, or glory! As a matter of fact, John said he. . . heard the voice of many angels around the throne and the living creatures and the elders; and the number of them was myriads of myriads, and thousands of thousands, saying with a loud voice,
> *Worthy is the Lamb that was slain to receive **power** and **riches** and **wisdom** and **might** and **honor** and **glory** and **blessing**.*

And every created thing which is in heaven and on the earth, and under the earth and on the sea, and all things in them saying,
> *To Him who sits on the throne, and to the Lamb, Be **blessing** and **honor** and **glory** and **dominion forever and ever**.*

And the four living creatures kept saying, Amen![5]

So should we!

Notes

1. White, *Testimonies to the Church* 9 : 109.
2. White, *Evangelism*, 122-123.
3. White, *Testimony to the Church* 6: 476.
4. This statement was made at a news conference on July 1, 2000 at the Adventist World Session 2000, Toronto Canada.
5. Revelation 5:11-14, NASB.

Appendix

THE NETWORK DISCIPLING MODEL

*I*n the world of business, one of the greatest challenges facing any industry is that of finding the right vehicle to move its goods and services to the customers who need them, in the fastest and most economical manner. In the attempt to accomplish this, traditional marketing distribution follows a series of steps, sometimes called the "distribution chain"—for example, manufacturer ➢ wholesaler ➢ retailer ➢ customer (or some other variation of middle managers between the manufacturer and the end-user).

However, a very powerful form of distribution that has virtually wiped out middle managers from the distribution chain can be found in the compelling force of network marketing, performed by Multilevel Marketing (MLM) corporations. These MLM companies recruit independent distributors, who make monthly purchases at a discounted price directly from the company. They also sell purchased products directly to their own customer base and earn commissions on people they recruit for the company. These new recruits also become independent distributors and basically repeat the same cycle of activity as the person who sponsored, or recruited them.

Through this process of duplication, these companies are able to generate millions of dollars each year, and at the same time, expand their customer base in an exponential manner. For example, a very close friend of mine has generated a network of business partners (called "downline") totaling over 6,000 people for her MLM company. I know of many others having groups of several hundreds working below them, generating astonishing sales volume for their respective companies, while at the same time recruiting many more people.

I would like to suggest that this powerful phenomenon of network marketing reflects the vision and philosophy of the greatest leader and teacher this world has ever known—Jesus Christ. I believe that this basic concept of networking was initiated by Jesus when He began His earthly ministry in Galilee. The Savior's challenge was very similar to that of any manufacturer of goods and services: "How could I get all these wonderful things that I have created to the world of customers who need them?" For Jesus, it was "How could I get this good news of My Father's love to a world of sinners who will certainly perish if they do not understand or receive it?" Christ's strategy was very simple. He called twelve common, everyday men, and trained them to become fishermen—that is, in the real sense of the word, fishers-of-men. Through these unlearned (according to the educational standards of the day) men, whom He called His disciples, and the simplest form of *leadership duplication* and *disciple networking*, Christ intended to reach the world of lost sinners. Christianity today is no longer confined to the regions around Palestine where it all began, but has become a growing global network of fishers-of-men, storming the kingdoms of darkness for Christ.

However, the sad truth is that Christianity has not built upon nor refined the Savior's network discipling strategy as marketers and MLM corporations have so efficiently done. While these merchants of the world are daily drawing countless thousands into their businesses to distribute and sell their products at unprecedented rates and generate extraordinary profits, many churches across the landscape of Christianity are daily struggling to draw new disciples into God's distribution system, to get the gospel to the perishing world.

It is because of this unwelcome reality and my startling discoveries in my experimentation with network marketing, that I am driven to propose the use of the concept of Network Discipling for the Kingdom of God in these last days. Here I will only present a mere sketch of this explosive evangelistic phenomenon, and will leave all the exciting details (the *what* and *how to*) for my next volume, "The Explosive Power of Network Discipling," that will shortly follow this one.

APPENDIX

DISCIPLING STUDY GUIDE

MISSION OBJECTIVES:
1. Produce fruit-bearing disciples
2. Develop compassionate, spiritual leaders
3. Generate growing small groups and churches
4. Build caring Christian communities

DISCIPLESHIP MOTTO:
Controlled by the Mind of Christ, Constrained by the Love of Christ, and Empowered by the Spirit of Christ.

CORE PHILOSOPHY:
1. **Understanding the Call – Matthew 4:17-19**
   a. Called to discipleship, not to membership
   b. Called to follow, not to fish
   c. Called to serve, not to sit

2. **Understanding the Cost – Luke 9:23-26**
   a. Forsaking All
   b. Denying of self
   c. Carrying the cross – losing the life

3. **Understanding the Command – Matthew 28:19, 20**
   a. Commissioned to Disciple-making

      b. Commissioned to all nations
      c. Commissioned to baptize and teach

4. **Understanding the Process – Matthew 4:19**
      a. Christ's Method alone (*Ministry of Healing*, 143)
      b. Disciple Duplication – Follow Me!

CORE STRATEGY:
1. **Make Disciples – Matthew 28:19, 20**
      a. Divine mandate
      b. Christ's Methods Alone/*3E Strategy
      c. Discipling Units/Cells

2. **Train Disciples – Matthew 5 - 7:29**
      a. The Disciple & his Master (Matthew 10:24, 25)
      b. Terms of discipleship (Luke 9:23-27)
      c. Spiritual formation – developing the mind and heart of Christ
      d. Kingdom Network Strategy
      e. *3E Strategy

3. **Deploy Disciples -- Matthew 10; Luke 10:1-16**
      a. Target Family – biological & spiritual (Lost Sheep of Israel)
      b. Target Friends – building social & spiritual bonds

c. Target Strangers – initiating & forming kingdom friendships

4. **Affirm Disciples – Luke 10:17-24**
   a. Power for Living sessions.
   b. Discipleship Challenge – Corporate worship and call to service (Weekly)
   c. Monthly Assessment – Discipling reports, goals & strategic planning
   d. Quarterly DDS – Discipleship Development Seminar – motivational seminars & workshops
   e. Truth Encounter Classes – TE111 & TE112

Note:

*3E Strategy:
   Expand - your friendship circle
   Expose - your friends to the love of Jesus
   Explain - to your friends to reason for your JOY

More Exciting Titles
by Dr. Ruthven J. Roy

The Samson Xfile

The Samson Xfile is the intriguing review of the most misunderstood faith-hero in the Bible—Samson. Christian tradition has perpetuated a negative view of this God-warrior; but the mysterious Xfile (Judges 14:4) of God's providence paints an amazingly very different picture. See your life reflected in God's dealing with Samson.

ISBN: 978-0-9717853-2-8 (Paperback)

The Explosive Power of Network Discipling

"Every Christian is called to be a disciple of Jesus; and every disciple is called to be a fisher, not just a member!" In this volume Dr. Roy clearly explains Christ's master plan for growing His kingdom. Christ calls everyone to discipleship, not membership.

ISBN: 978-0-9717853-4-2

Imitating God

Imitating God is not only possible, but it is also guaranteed. This book will make available to you the key to your true identity, and will show you, in very simple steps, how to unleash the power of God's life from within you. Get ready to enter into the **God-zone**.

ISBN: 978-0-9717853-3-5

Study Guide: Imitating God

Do not forget this companion Study Guide to go along with this magnificent text. It would greatly enhance your understanding of all the vital issues that pertain to your spiritual identity and living victoriously. Moreover, this Study Guide will provide you with an exciting, hands-on way to share this good news with others.

ISBN: 978-0-9717853-6-6

Unshakeable Kingdom

In the church, yet outside of God's kingdom! What a tragedy! Learn how to avoid the "Nicodemus Syndrome," the common sickness of modern Christianity! Understand true kingdom fitness and why religion is simply not enough. ***The kingdom of heaven is NOW; not later! Later is TOO late!*** This volume will change your focus and your life in a way that only a miracle from God can. ***Seize the moment, and make the decision to enter God's Unshakeable Kingdom now!***

ISBN: 978-0-9717853-3-5

Position Yourself for Success

God knew and wrote our success story long before our arrival on this planet. True success depends on how we position ourselves in relation to God's purpose for our existence in this world. This book will help you to discover and pursue it!

ISBN: 978-0-9717853-8-0

Born-Again Life

Born-again life is not an upgrade or a transformation of our life in Adam, but a total replacement of it. This life, though expressed through our physical humanity, has not a thread of humanity in it. It is absolutely incorruptible and totally divine, because it originated directly from the incorruptible God. If your born-again experience is everything else but exciting, restful, victorious and totally satisfying, then this book is guaranteed to be an abundant, life-transforming blessing to you.

ISBN: 978-0-9717853-9-7

Available online or at your local Christian bookstore

For more information, visit www.roybooks.com, or write to
Rehoboth Publishing, P.O. Box 33, Berrien Springs, MI 49103

Contact Information

Dr. Ruthven J. Roy

NETWORK DISCIPLING MINISTRIES
P.O. Box 33
Berrien Springs, MI 49103

Tel: (301) 514-2383
Email: ruthvenroy@gmail.com

RUTHVEN ROY is a discipleship consultant and founder of Network Discipling Ministries. He and his wife Lyris live in Michigan, and are the parents of three precious daughters—Charisa, Lyrisa and Mirisa.

www.ingramcontent.com/pod-product-compliance
Lightning Source LLC
Chambersburg PA
CBHW071944110426
42744CB00030B/289